BROOKLYN'S
BAY RIDGE and FORT HAMILTON

a photographic journey

1870 - 1970

BRIAN MERLIS and LEE A. ROSENZWEIG

published by

Israelowitz Publishing

in association with

Brooklyn Editions

2000

ACKNOWLEDGMENTS

The authors gratefully appreciate the generous assistance offered to them by the following individuals:
Jack and Rita Merlis, Sidney and Henny Rosenzweig, Robert L. Presbrey, Ronald Marzlock, Jimmy Charles, Richard Hyland, William McManus, Kevin Walsh and his website forgotten-ny.com, Louis Castaldo, Robert and Helene Stonehill, Allen Kent, and Joy Holland of the Brooklyn Public Library. Special thanks go to Jimmy at Bay Ridge Film Center, and to Ray Flood and Jim Clark of Flood Agency. Assisting in the editorial process were Sharon Miller, Laura Moskowitz, and Ken Kimmel. Special thanks go to Eli, Peter, Bona, and Steve at East Coast Camera in Valley Stream for their patience and quality photo reproduction work.

We especially want to thank the people of Bay Ridge and Fort Hamilton for their willingness to share their knowledge and memories of their neighborhoods with us. The authors apologize for any factual or typographical errors which may have occurred during this endeavor.
Brian & Lee

Copyright 2000 by Brian Merlis and Lee A. Rosenzweig
All rights reserved under Pan American and
International Copyright Conventions.

Reproduction in whole or part without permission of the authors is prohibited. Under Sections 107 and 108 of the U. S. Copyright Law, no part of this publication may be reproduced, stored in a retrieval system, or transmitted, in any form, or by any means, electronic, mechanical, photocopying, recording, or otherwise, without the prior permission of the authors.

All photographs, maps, and illustrations from the collections of Brian Merlis, Lee A. Rosenzweig, Robert and Helene Stonehill, and Robert L. Presbrey.

Published by Israelowitz Publishing,
P O Box 228, Brooklyn, NY 11229
tel. & fax: (718) 951-7072
E-Mail: oscari477@aol.com
and
Brooklyn Editions, P O Box 14, Lynbrook, NY
11563 tel: (516) 593-4505
foreverbklyn@juno.com
foreverbklyn@mindspring.com

This book was designed by the authors.
Cover photographs colorized by Brian Merlis
Printed and bound in The United States of America

International Standard Book Number: 1-878741-45-4
L - C - Control Number: 00132427

INTRODUCTION

BAY RIDGE-FORT HAMILTON, with its spectacular views of New York Bay, sits as a brilliant jewel in the crown of Brooklyn neighborhoods. The high bluffs formed from rock deposits moving along the outer edge of the last great glacier, receding thousands of years ago, creating Long Island and the Hudson River. Cool breezes blowing from nearby New York Bay and the Atlantic Ocean make it an ideal location on hot summer nights.

The first known settlers were of Mongolian descent and were known as the *Lenape*. It was these early natives who watched the first Europeans arrive in the New World in great sailing ships. Two famous explorers were Giovanni da Verrazano, an Italian who sailed for the heir to the throne of France, and Henry Hudson, an Englishman who sailed for the Dutch East India Company from the Netherlands. It was the Dutch who in 1652 bought the Bay Ridge-Fort Hamilton area from the Nyack Indians. This sleepy Dutch settlement, originally called Yellow Hook for the yellow clay found in its soil, became British with the capture of New Amsterdam in 1664. The British lined the communities in the present Borough of Brooklyn into one administrative unit called Kings County in the Province of New York, in 1683.

The American Revolution shook up this gentle farming community when American General Henry Knox shelled the British as they mounted their campaign in the Battle of Brooklyn in August of 1776 from the heights of Bay Ridge in the town of New Utrecht. The Narrows assumed military importance on a national level from that time on. The first military fortification, Fort Lewis, built of mud and wood, protected New York City from invasion during the War of 1812. It was replaced by Fort Hamilton, a magnificent granite structure built from 1825 to 1831. Fort Hamilton played an instrumental role in quelling the 1863 Civil War draft riots in New York City. Later it was used as a major embarkation center for troops going to Europe in both World Wars. It now serves the community by giving a home to a major US Veterans Administration Hospital and to the 26th Army Band. The reputation Bay Ridge has as a center of fine restaurants and a swinging night life began with the early hostelries and taverns which sprung up around Fort Hamilton to serve its troops.

As New York's metropolitan area became an industrial center in the latter half of the nineteenth century, Bay Ridge became one of its residential communities attracting Europeans of Scandinavian, German, Irish, and Italian descent. The Farrell House, now landmarked, contains a widows walk, a balcony where seamen's wives would pace as they searched for their husbands' ships in the nearby ocean. As wealth concentrated in New York, Bay Ridge-Fort Hamilton was sought as a prime location for the mansions and institutions of the elite. Lavish homes were built along what is now Shore Road. The Crescent Athletic Club became a center of the high life of the upper classes. The present-day Fontbonne Academy For Girls was the home of actress Lillian Russell and investment banker "Diamond Jim" Brady. Elegant restaurants and fine shops were built to serve this community.

In the twentieth century, as the wealthy moved to new locations, middle- class homes grew along Bay Ridge's beautiful tree-lined, hill-climbing streets. Savory sea food became a trademark of good eating in Bay Ridge. Fourth Avenue, Fifth Avenue, and 86th Street became commercial centers reflecting in its shops the community's ethnic diversity. The greatest change to Bay Ridge-Fort Hamilton in the twentieth century came with the construction of the Verrazano-Narrows Bridge from 1959 to 1964. Originally opposed by its residents, the bridge now stands as a symbol of both neighborhood unity and ethnic pride. In 1964, with the changes in immigration law, new residents began to arrive from The Balkans, Greece, The Middle East and Eastern Asia. The newest arrivals in the 1990s came from China and the former Soviet Union. Night life in Bay Ridge became world famous with the release of the movie Saturday Night Fever. Sine 1976, the New York City Marathon has begun from the Verrazano-Narrows Bridge with the runners moving along neighborhood streets to the cheers of the crowds. Television has captured the breathtaking views of Staten Island and the Manhattan skyline for all the world to see from Bay Ridge.

For centuries, Bay Ridge-Fort Hamilton has been a special place to live with a rich history and many diverse cultural influences. It has played a role in the development of New York City, New York State, and the United States of America. With an appreciation of its glorious past, Bay Ridge-Fort Hamilton looks forward to the third millennium. **Bay Ridge-Fort Hamilton**— may you continue to be a bright jewel shining upon our future!

I. Stephen Miller,
President
Sheepshead Bay Historical Society

Brooklyn's Bay Ridge and Fort Hamilton, neighboring villages within the former Town of New Utrecht, lie on Long Island's westernmost point. Fort Hamilton is situated between the Narrows, Dyker Meadows, and approximately 87th Street. Bay Ridge extends northward to the old Brooklyn city line (59th - 60th Streets), and eastward to approximately Tenth Avenue, at Dyker Heights. During the twentieth century, residents of South Brooklyn within the former city limits, considered themselves Bay Ridge residents. Some have included the Finnish colony surrounding Sunset Park, up to Green-Wood Cemetery (37th Street), to be part of Bay Ridge.

The bluff overlooking New York Bay and continuing eastward is part of the glacial terminal moraine—Long Island's backbone, formed during the last Ice Age. Beds of wampum, or shells, discovered near the site of Fort Hamilton, strongly suggest that this locale was often visited by the Canarsee and Nyack tribes of Native Americans.

Giovanni da Verrazano, the Florentine navigator, was the first European to view Long Island. In April 1524, aboard the French caravel *Dauphine*, he sailed through the Narrows in search of a transcontinental passage. Verrazano described his entrance into the great harbor: "...we found a very agreeable situation located within two small hills, in the midst of which flowed into the sea a very great river, which was deep within the mouth;"

In 1609, Henry Hudson, representing the Dutch East India Company, sailed into the harbor aboard the *Halve Maen (Half Moon)*, with a crew of eighteen. At that time, the bay was filled with fish and shellfish. The land was inhabited by wildlife, including bears. As late as November 26, 1759, a large bear, trying to swim from Red Hook to New Utrecht, was shot by a Brooklyn man named Sebring.

In 1638, Dutch Governor-General Willem Kieft bought a tract, including *Hamel's Hooftden*, from Penhawitz, then the great chief of the Canarsees. *Hamel's Hooftden* referred to the highlands of Staten Island and Bay Ridge. They were named *Hooftden* due to their resemblance to the shores of *Hooftden* (meaning headlands of the channel) between Dover, England and Calais, France. Hamel was a director of the Dutch West India Company.

In 1639, Heer Antony van Salee (a.k.a. Anthony Jansen or Johnson) became the first individual to apply for a land grant in the area. Salee, born in Fez, Morocco, was one of New Amsterdam's first African-American settlers. In 1643, Governor-General Kieft granted Salee title retroactive to 1639 for 100 morgens (about 200 acres) located at the New Utrecht-Gravesend border, near today's Twenty-third Avenue. In 1660, Salee sold his land to Nicholas Stillwell, and returned to New Amsterdam, where he died about 1676.

Cornelis van Werckhoven, Alderman of Utrecht on the banks of the Rhine, member of the Netherlands Government, and influential in the Dutch West India Company, announced he would colonize the *Hooftden*. Arriving with Augustus Heermans as land agent and Jacques Cortelyou, a French Huguenot, as his children's tutor, he purchased 180 acres in 1652, including the Nyack Indian Village (present-day Fort Hamilton). A true Renaissance man, Cortelyou was a linguist, mathematician, philosopher, and surveyor.

When van Werckhoven went to claim his property, other Indians had taken up residence there, denying knowledge of any prior sale by Penhawitz. Cornelis van Werckhoven had to buy the land again, and the deed for the property, dated November 22, 1652, is still on file in the Kings County Clerk's office. The repurchase included additional lands, totaling slightly over one thousand acres. The Indians charged the Dutch more for New Utrecht than had been accepted for all of Manhattan!

Van Werckhoven returned to Holland to recruit settlers, but died there in 1655. This left Cortelyou in charge of the fledgling settlement.

In 1657, Dutch settlers purchased more land from the Indians and established the Town of New Utrecht, named after van Werckhoven's home town. For their protection, the Dutch built a "long house" just within the entrance of today's Fort Hamilton Reservation. Jacques Cortelyou, recognized by Governor Peter Stuyvesant for his leadership qualities, was the main founder of the Dutch settlement. When the small village was destroyed by fire in 1675, Stuyvesant sent workmen to rebuild the Cortelyou house. His old log house, located at Fort Hamilton, was rebuilt out of stone. Early settlers built dykes on the edge of what were then acres of meadows, now Dyker Beach Park.

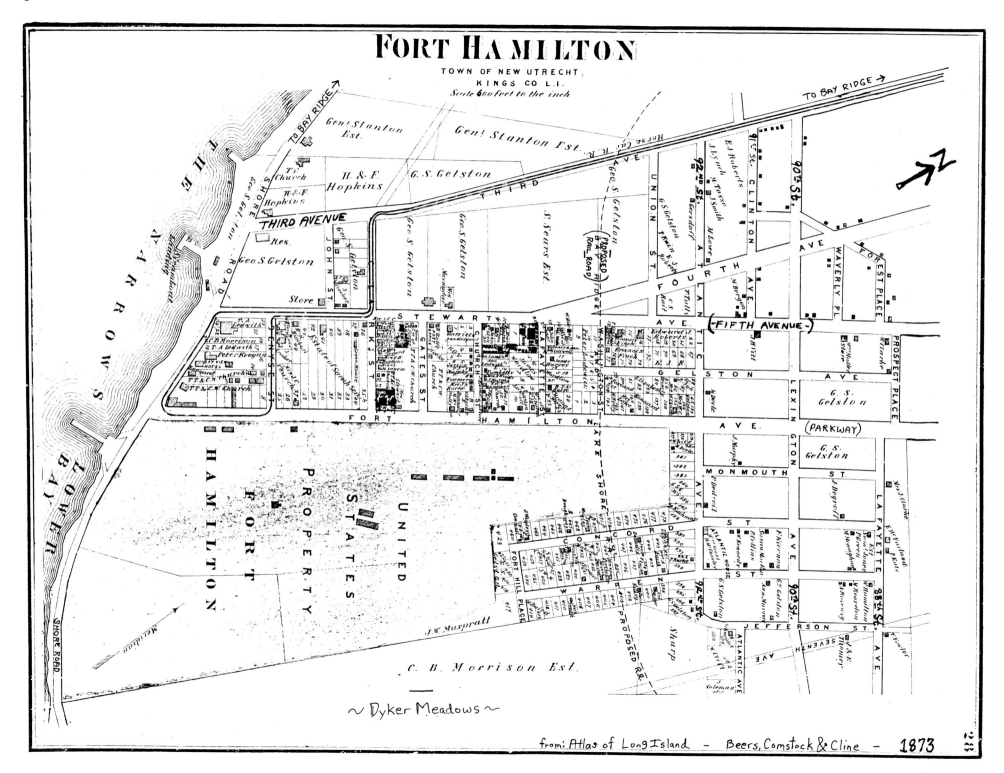

All of the property along today's Shore Road was quickly acquired by the early Dutch settlers. The road, first mentioned in 1715, was described as twenty-two yards wide, extending from today's Bay Ridge Avenue to Bath Beach.

The New Utrecht Reformed Church was organized in October 1677 at 84th Street (Kings Highway) and Sixteenth Avenue. In 1827, stones from the original church were used to rebuild the present church at Eighteenth Avenue at 84th Street. A branch of this church, the Bay Ridge Dutch Reformed Church (Union Church), was later (1896) built at 80th Street and Ridge Boulevard on farmland donated by Jaques Van Brunt.

The remote agricultural community of Yellow Hook experienced a slow pace of growth during Colonial times, whereas a faster rate of population growth and agricultural activity took place in and around the village of New Utrecht, centered near today's 84th Street between Sixteenth and Nineteenth Avenues. Settlers spent their time clearing forests, constructing homesteads, planting vegetables, grain, and tobacco, and raising cattle, while limiting interaction with the natives. Farmers relied heavily on the use of manure, since the soil of Yellow Hook and much of New Utrecht was Miami stony loam, best suited to grow grasses and grain, such as corn and wheat.

In 1663, a motley crew of Englishmen, led by Captain John Scott, raided New Utrecht. Seventy horsemen and sixty infantry, clothed in civilian array, sailed from Connecticut into the English-controlled eastern reaches of Long Island. They then clattered toward the peaceful Dutch towns on the west end. Although there was no war between Holland and England, Captain Scott proclaimed himself President of the English Towns of Long Island. Led by this Puritan-guerilla, the band of raiders marched into New Utrecht, threatening settlers, and even drawing a sword upon the ailing body of Mrs. Rutgert Joosten Van Brunt. The surrounding townspeople interceded to prevent her death. As Dutch-Governor Stuyvesant began to mobilize his troops, Scott and his regiment retreated eastward. Stuyvesant launched a letter of protest to Scott and to the Crown, but after Dutch investigators interviewed Scott and found him arrogant, they ended the interrogation, and let their governments in Europe settle the matter.

On December 8, 1664, a fleet bearing the English flag appeared in Gravesend Bay. With reinforcements from Eastern Long Island and New England, Stuyvesant was forced to surrender New Amsterdam to the English.

Under English Governor Nicolls' administration, the town's existing patents were recognized and rewritten under the British Crown. Although a name change was considered, *Nieuw Utrecht* was able to retain its Dutch name.

After England and France declared war on Holland in March 1672, a Dutch fleet entered New York Bay on July 29th, seizing the colony after nearly nine years of English rule. One month later, all 41 New Utrecht residents formally swore their allegiance to Holland.

On August 8, 1673, the west end of Long Island, previously designated by the English as The West Riding of Yorkshire, was reorganized as Kings County, under a new charter, by Governor Colve. The war ended with the signing of the Treaty of Westminster on February 19, 1674. On August 27th and 28th of that year, a British fleet anchored in Gravesend Bay. Colonel Nicoll demanded and obtained the surrender of New Netherlands from Stuyvesant. That was the last time the Dutch flag ever flew over New Netherlands. The surrender took place just off the present Fort Hamilton.

During the 1679 visit from Holland by Dankers and Sluyter, two Labadist monks, the Narrows was boarded by numerous Nyack Indians, with canoes full of fruit for sale. Being warmly greeted, the Dutchmen visited the natives' wigwam, which stood near today's Fort Hamilton. They found seven or eight families of the tribe living in one hut, eating ground maize. The visitors were seated before great fires, and were served peaches, melons, and other strange and exotic fruit.

Although African slaves were owned by Bay Ridge's landowners, a few free blacks also resided in the area. In addition to original patentee Antony van Salee, Swan von Tuane from Sierre Leone purchased a large farm at Owl's Head (today's 69th Street) in 1670, shortly after obtaining his freedom. A member of the gentry, his two daughters were baptized in the Dutch Reformed Church of New Utrecht.

By 1698, 259 people resided in the Town of New Utrecht, including 48 slaves. Thirty years later, 282 dwelled there, including 119 slaves. By 1755, the slave population had dropped to 67, and by the late 1820s, all Kings County slaves had been manumitted.

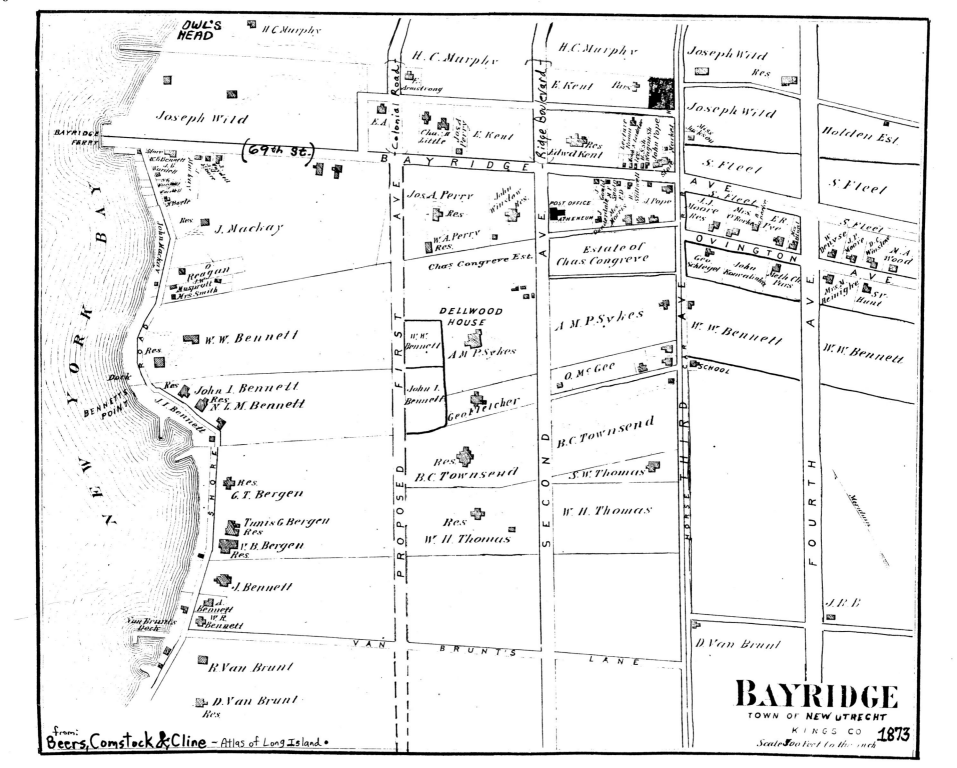

A town militia was organized about 1698, commanded by Captain John Van Dyke.

On February 14, 1702, a winter white oak tree was designated the official boundary between Brooklyn and New Utrecht. In 1845, surveyor Teunis G. Bergen placed a stone monument in the decaying stump of that famous tree, to further mark the easterly angle of the borderline.

In 1742, King George granted Denyse Denyse permission to operate a ferry. The first documented use of this franchise occurred in 1753 when Thomas Stilwell and/or John Lane began operation, probably leasing from Denyse the rights and dock at the foot of Van Brunt's Lane (today's 79th Street). The rowboat took passengers to and from Staten Island and Brooklyn Ferry. An ardent patriot, Denyse was later chosen as a delegate to the Provincial Congress at New York (April 1775), assembled to voice resistance to British oppression.

Prior to the outbreak of the Revolution, occupying British troops were often seen in town. They were quartered all over Kings County for the seven years prior to 1776. Some joined the American ranks. Occasional personal conflicts and quarrels took place between the troops and the townsfolk. The British kept an eye on the granaries, cattle, and crops.

A few weeks prior to the appearance of the British fleet, a party of Americans established a battery of two or three twelve-pound guns at Denyse's Ferry.

On June 29, 1776, 45 ships were sighted off Coney Island. The Patriots feared that the British might try to land at Gravesend, but they mobilized on Staten Island instead. By mid July, 437 British ships, under General William Howe's command, were anchored off Staten Island. Although George Washington believed that an attack upon New Utrecht was imminent, Howe was waiting for his brother, Richard, who was en route from England with 150 ships and 20,000 more soldiers, and for General Clinton, with 2,500 troops which had just defeated the Americans at Charleston.

Teunis G. Bergen, in Stiles' 1884 *History of Kings County,* writes: "The first resistance made to the British arms in the Middle States of America, was on the soil of New Utrecht, near where the present Fort Hamilton stands." On August 22, 1776, without waiting for an attack, the Americans opened fire on the frigate *HMS Asia,* which headed Lord Howe's fleet. The British rapidly returned the volley. According to an account in a Philadelphia newspaper, the Bennett house was hit by a 24-pound cannonball from the Battleship *Asia*, which was riding close to the shore in the rear of the British fleet. The Honorable Teunis G. Bergen owned several of the cannon balls which struck his ancestors' homestead, but lost them and other relics in the Fulton & Flatbush Storage Co.'s fire, about 1875. The old Bennett homestead stood until the middle of the twentieth century.

According to a 1910 account by family historian Peter L. Cortelyou, his ancestor, Nancy Corteljau, upon seeing the British soldiers land near the present-day Dyker Beach Park, impulsively rushed out on the high ground near her home. As a Tory, she enthusiastically waved southward to them, using her red petticoat as a flag (knowing that red was the British color). The 16,000 British soldiers responded to her welcome on that historic morning of August 22, 1776, almost immediately, taking possession of the surrounding neighborhood. However, Dr. Lawrence B. Cortelyou claimed in 1893 that his ancestors were not Tories, but "Neutrals."

When the British landed at Bay Ridge, an old black man was forced to ride some of the King's soldiers up the hill in his dump cart. When he reached his master's (Stanton) farmhouse at today's 98th Street at Shore Road, the slave quickly dumped them into the roadway as he drove into the barnyard. The Stanton farmhouse stood until about 1940.

Several of the occupying forces entered Colonel William J. Cropsey's grandmother's (Phebe Emans) house on Kings Highway where they devoured all the freshly baked food she had prepared for her family. The English troops subsequently raided the cellar and took all they could find.

According to Mrs. Bleecker Bangs, in her 1912 *Reminiscences of Old New Utrecht and Gowanus,* the English confiscated and ruined much during their occupancy of the farmhouses and buildings. Residents were compelled to take an oath of allegiance, hated by the great majority, yet necessary if home and family were to be saved. The British soldiers took the best of everything and at once domiciled themselves in the homes of the helpless New Utrecht residents, who dared not rebel.

BATTLE OF BROOKLYN

However, on the morning after their landing, the British and Hessian troops encountered limited American resistance near what is now Third and Ovington Avenues. The Patriots were no match, and the King's forces continued their occupation of New Utrecht, mobilizing their forces and advancing north. The Battle of Brooklyn would occur several days later, on August 27, 1776.

During the Revolution, a Cortelyou daughter fell in love with a young Hessian officer and secretly married him. The girl's family, angered by the romance, separated the lovers, and the groom left the house and shot himself on a bluff overlooking the Narrows. The young bride later died of a broken heart.

On Tuesday, April 20, 1790, teachers at New Utrecht's little red schoolhouse told all students to "hurry home, scrub your faces and hands, put on your Sunday best, and get back as fast as you can." When they returned, they lined up outside the school and saw a coach with four horses and outriders approaching. When the cavalcade reached the students, a tall gentleman stepped out. George Washington shook hands with each child. When he came to the last boy the President said: "Peter, if you are a good boy, you will grow up to be a great and good man." Peter van Pelt became a respected minister.

This story, passed down from father to son, may not be completely accurate. Although Washington did record a visit to the town in his diary, he made no mention of the school children. In addition, the pupils may not have understood all of Washington's words since he spoke English and they spoke Dutch. Four years later, in 1794, Jacques Barkaloo ran a newspaper advertisement calling for "a school teacher capable of teaching the English language." The population of New Utrecht at this time was about 600.

According to Bergen, when Bay Ridge and Fort Hamilton entered the nineteenth century, "the new (American) laws and spirit became prevalent and the Dutch language began to lose its prominence, until it remained only a historic treasure reverently guarded in every home, and used constantly as a means of secrecy, or as a band of intimacy, under the sway of the more opulent English tongue."

At this time, Shore Road was bordered with cherry trees. Passers-by would often pick the fruit which hung over the road.

Documented by Moreau de St. Menz, visiting from France (1793-1798), a pleasure resort was established on the waterfront in the late 1700s. A sea-bathing house was standing on the shore in 1794 which boasted an 18- by 45-foot dining room. Numerous picnics were held there, and a palm was awarded to the person who could drink the most. The bath house described by Moreau de St. Menz was probably located at Bath Beach. The "semi-sanitarium" was supervised by Drs. Bailey, Bard, Rogers, and Tillary. It burned down in 1802. The original Hamilton House (ca. 1820) was the first major resort hotel at the Narrows.

In 1792, a speculator named Richard M. Woodhull purchased property in the northwest section of the town of Bushwick, near the Wallabout. Woodhull hired Colonel Jonathan Williams, a military engineer, to survey his land. Woodhull named the area after his surveyor, calling it Williamsburgh. Fifteen years later, in 1807, Williams suggested the establishment of an artillery battery to be built on Hendrick's Reef, a small rock island off Denyse's Ferry. Rejected initially, it was not until the War of 1812 that his proposal was seriously considered. Called Fort Diamond due to its shape, the fort was built between 1812 and 1822. On March 25, 1823, it was renamed Fort Lafayette in commemoration of Major General Lafayette's services during the Revolution.

During the Civil War, the fort was used as a prison for Northern rebels. Hawley D. Clapp was able to see his home through the casement window of his prison cell at Fort Lafayette. Robert Cobb Kennedy, a Confederate spy who tried to burn down New York City, was hanged from Fort Lafayette's gallows on March 25, 1865, three weeks prior to Lincoln's assassination. A great fire occurred at Fort Lafayette in 1868. Miraculously, tons of stored gunpowder failed to explode during the blaze.

FORT HAMILTON. 1889

PUBLIC OFFICES, CHURCHES, ETC.

POST OFFICE—Stewart av n Gates, Adrian M. Stillwell, Postmaster.

TOWN HALL—86th n Fort Hamilton av, Patrick Drurey, Keeper.

CHURCHES—St. John's (*Protestant Episcopal*), Fort Hamilton av c Clarke, Rev. Robert B. Snowden. (*Reformed Dutch*), Stewart av n Clarke. St. Patrick's (*Roman Catholic*), Stewart av c Lafayette, Rev. John Tanzer.

SCHOOL HOUSE—No. 4.

NEW UTRECHT BUILDING & LOAN ASSOCIATION.

FIRE DEPARTMENT—Engine No. 1, junc. 4th & 5th avs.

U. S. MILITARY POST—Alex Piper, Colonel; Albert Hartsuff, Major and Post Surgeon; Abram C. Wildrich, Major; Anthony W. Vodges, 1st Lt., R. and P. Q. M.; W. B. McCallum, 1st Lt., R. and P. Adjt.

INEBRIATES HOME—3d av n 89th st, office 12 Boerum pl, B'klyn.

MISCELLANEOUS SOCIETIES—U. S. A. & N. Vet. Fred Hastings, Captain, meets at Doyle's House, 92 n Fort Hamilton av.

AGENT, REAL ESTATE.
Tasso Constantine, 92d n 3d av

BLACKSMITH.
Lake Joseph, John n Stewart av

BOATS TO LET.
Gates P. & M. Shore rd n Stewart av
Hegeman Robert H. ft Stewart av
Stillwell Adrian, Shore rd n Fort Hamilton av

BOOTS AND SHOES.
Kluge Herman, 5th av n 86th

BOTTLER.
Mehl Charles, 91st & 5th av

Bottling Machinery & Supplies.
Wittemann Bros.

BUTCHERS.
Costello Patrick, Stewart av c Wash'n av
Grummet John, 5th av c Church
Mittnight Frank, 92d n 4th av

CARPENTERS.
Doyle Martin, 91st n 4th av
Emmons Robert, Denyse n Stewart av
Hastings & Albers, Fort Hamilton av n 92d
Tierny William J. 91st n 3d av

CARRIAGE MAKERS.
Penger Walter E. 86th n Fort Hamilton av
Statler Joseph, 88th n 4th av

CIGAR DEALERS.
Mehl Charles, 5th av n 91st
Meyer Ferdinand, Fort Hamilton av c Laf

CLERGYMEN.
Snowden Robt. B. Fort Hamilton av c Clarke
Tanzer John, Stewart av n Laf

CONFECTIONERS.
Finley Margaret, Fort Hamilton av n Shore rd
Flynn Annie, 5th av n 91st

CONTRACTORS.
McGlyn John, Church n Stewart av
McGlyn John, 90th & 4th av
Mitchell William, Stewart av n 4th av

COUNTRY STORES.
Berry Alphonso, Stewart av c Clarke
Brown William B. 5th av c 91st
Emmons Robert, Denyse n Stewart av
Slater Richard, Stewart av n Gates
Tasso Mary, 92d n 3d av

DRESSMAKERS.
Meyer Johanna, Fort Hamilton av c Laf
Rice Bridget, 92d n Concord

DRUGS.
Blankley William H. Stewart av c Clarke

EXPRESSES.
McKnight Michael, Stewart av c Laf
Westaway William A. Clarke n Stewart av

FISH.
Richman Arthur G. Warren c Laf
Smith W. J. Stewart av n Church

FANCY GOODS.
McGlyn Mary A. Stewart av n Church
Molloy Maria, 4th av c 88th

FRUITS.
Monahan John, Warren n 92d

GROCERS.
Bullock Elizabeth, 91st n 3d av
Butsch Julius, 4th av c 88th
Clarke William, 5th av c Prospect pl
Emmons Robert, Denyse n Stewart av
Farrell Mary, 3d av n 91st
Kelly Joseph, Fort Hamilton av c Church
Lake Alonzo A. Stewart av c John
Lester & Doyle, 91st n 4th av
Muller William, 5th av c 89th
Otton Anne, 5th av n 91st

HAIRDRESSER.
Folsom Sylvester M. Clarke n Stewart av

HORSESHOER.
Lake Joseph, John n Stewart av

HOTELS.
Bay View House, James Keegan, Shore rd
Brooklyn House, Carl Nealsson, Stewart av n Denyse
Connolly's M. Shore ft Stewart av
Grand View
Haas Otto, 86th n Town Hall
Live Oak, 92d c Concord
Newman House, John Hunt, Stewart av c Denyse
Ocean Hotel, Harry B. Johnson, Fort Hamilton av c Shore rd
Sea View, John Nappier, Shore rd n Fort Hamilton
United States, Michael Gates, Shore rd n Stewart av

ICE DEALERS.
Brady Philip, 90th n 4th av
Clark Thomas J. 5th av n 88th
McNally Bros. Clarke n Stewart av

LIQUORS.
Burke Patrick, 92d n Concord
Cropsy James V. 86th n 7th av
Drury Thomas, Denyse n Stewart av
Duffy Frank, 92d n Concord
Flannagan T. P. 4th av n 88th
Kirk John W. Fort Hamilton av n Gates
Leydet Joseph, Fort Hamilton av c Church
Mang Frederick, 92d n 4th av
Martin Henry, Denyse n Stewart av
Mehl Charles, 91st & 5th av
Monaghan Michael, Warren n Laf
Smith James F. 86th n Fort Hamilton av
Taylor Joseph P. 4th av c 94th
Wynne James B. 3d av n 91st

MASON.
McGlyn John, Stewart av c Church

MILK.
Coyle Patrick, Warren n 92d
Hickman Thomas, 91st n 4th av
McCarty John, 3d av

NURSE.
McBride Mary, 3d av n Lex av

OILS.
Carroll Lawrence, Warren n Lex av

PAINTERS.
Maxwell & Wilson, 3d av n 91st

PHYSICIAN.
Thorne H. S. 96th & Shore rd

TAILOR.
Katzenberger John, Concord n 92d

TELEGRAPH CO.
Western Union, Fort Hamilton n Shore rd

TOBACCO AND CIGARS.
Mehl Charles, 5th av n 91st

SAMUEL HARTELIUS,
PAINTER AND PAPER HANGER,
KALSOMINING, WOOD FINISHING,
79th Street, Near Fifth Avenue,
BAY RIDGE, BROOKLYN, N. Y.

SEND FOR ESTIMATE.

The government obtained title to land bordering on the Narrows in May 1814, and a one-acre fort was soon built there, originally known as Fort Lewis. Many years later it was renamed Fort Hamilton in honor of Treasury Secretary Alexander Hamilton. Construction of the fort's main section began in April 1825, and ended six years later. Built on lands ceded to the government in 1824, the quadrangular fort is built of gray granite, and has two defenses—one for water and another for land.

According to Hoffman's *The Bay Ridge Chronicles* (1976), the construction of the fort ushered in an era of economic prosperity in New Utrecht. Nearly half a million dollars were spent on the fort's construction. Wharves were built along the shore for the landing of supplies. By 1843, the water defense boasted fourteen casements and twenty-six barbettes, thirty-two pounders, and thirty-two large-caliber casement guns.

In 1841, Robert E. Lee, a young Virginian, was named Fort Hamilton's Post Engineer. During his five-year tenure, he modified Staten Island's Fort Wadsworth and other nearby military installations. His house still stands on the fort grounds.

Moving out of the house when superiors needed a residence, Lee rented a room in the James Church house, across Smith Avenue (later United States Avenue and now Fort Hamilton Parkway).

Thomas "Stonewall" Jackson came to Fort Hamilton after his 1846 graduation from West Point. After serving in the Mexican War, he was reassigned to Fort Hamilton as a major, residing in the Dillon Mansion on 99th Street.

Both Lee and Jackson were parishioners of St. John's Episcopal Church, where Lee sponsored Jackson's 1849 baptism.

Major General Abner Doubleday, credited with the invention of baseball, was post commander at Fort Hamilton during the outbreak of the Civil War (1861). He later became a hero at the Battle of Gettysburg.

The government base was enlarged to about 96 acres in 1891. Today the facility stands on 155 acres. During the World Wars, Fort Hamilton served as a major embarkation and separation center.

During World War II, pugilist Joe Louis taught boxing to troops at Fort Hamilton. Sergeant Louis gave exhibition bouts there in 1944 and 1945.

After World War II, the government built the Fort Hamilton Veterans' Hospital. The sixteen-story structure, completed in 1950, cost seventeen million dollars.

During the Cold War, the anti-ship guns were replaced by Nike missiles, harbor mines, and submarine nets.

The Fort Hamilton Historical Society was chartered in 1980. The Harbor Defense Museum was established at the fort's garrison at about the same time.

In 1997, Fort Hamilton came under the command of the Military District of Washington. The fort is now home to the New York City Recruiting Battalion, the Military Entrance Processing Station, and The North Atlantic Division Headquarters of the U.S. Army Corps of Engineers. The 26th Army Band and about 150 families are stationed at the base. Currently the nation's second-oldest continuously garrisoned federal post, Fort Hamilton continues to maintain 300 Reserve and National Guard Units.

Regular horse-drawn stage service between New Utrecht village and Fort Hamilton was begun in the 1830s by James Church. He also ran coaches to Brooklyn, along the Gowanus Road. Church's general store served as the village post office.

Due to the color of its soil and sand, the Bay Ridge-Fort Hamilton section had been known as *Geelen Hoeck*, or Yellow Hook, until about 1854. Beginning in 1848, several yellow fever epidemics, probably spread by infected sailors from merchant ships moored in the harbor, overtook the area, decimating the population. As a reaction to the negative association between the disease and the place name, the village fathers felt that a name change was necessary.

At a December 1853 meeting chaired by Teunis G. Bergen, and attended by such notables as Henry C. Murphy, Jaques Van Brunt, and others, a resolution, presented by florist James Weir, was unanimously passed, calling the locality **Bay Ridge**.

About the time of the name change, an artists' colony known as Ovington Village had been established between Third and Seventh Avenues from 72nd Street to Bay Ridge Avenue. Charles Parsons, art director of Harper & Bro., was the first president of the Ovington Village Association. Ovington Avenue was opened, and deep residential lots were mapped out along it. Joseph Perry built the first house there, and brothers Edward and Henry A. Kent each had

courtesy of Louis Castaldo

BAY RIDGE.

1889

PUBLIC OFFICES, CHURCHES, Etc.

POST OFFICE—2d av n Bay Ridge av, Wm. Wakefield, Postmaster.

CHURCHES—Grace (*Methodist Episcopal*), 4th av c Ovington av, Rev. John Pitkington. Christ's (*Protestant Episcopal*), Church la n 3d av, Rev. Wm. H. Morgan.

EDUCATIONAL DEPARTMENT—Public School No. 2, 2d av s of Cedar la.

FIRE DEPARTMENT—Bay Ridge Hook and Ladder Co., Bay Ridge av n 3d. Bay Ridge Engine Co., No. 1, 3d av n Bay Ridge av. Neptune Engine Co., No. 2, ft Bay Ridge av.

BAY RIDGE BRASS BAND—Athenæum, 2d av n Bay Ridge av, J. F. Hernandez, Leader.

RAILROADS—Long Island (formerly Manhattan Beach) ft 65th and 115 B'way N. Y. New York and Sea Beach, 65th and 3d av and 56 Wall, N. Y., Frank Jacobus, Sup't.

MISCELLANEOUS SOCIETIES—Bay Ridge and Fort Hamilton Citizen's Association, Athenæum. Meets monthly.

PUBLIC HALL—Athenæum, 2d av n Bay Ridge av.

AGENT, REAL ESTATE.
ERICKSON CHARLES A. Bay Ridge av n 3d av

BATHS.
Speck John, ft 67th

BOATS TO LET.
Wardell J. Henry, Shore rd n Bay Ridge av

BOOTS AND SHOES.
Erickson Charles A. Bay Ridge av n 3d av

BUTCHERS.
Gould John, Bay Ridge av n 3d av
Hemenway N. O. Bay Ridge av n 3d av
Kroeck Jacob. Stewart av cor Bay Ridge av
Ryder Samuel, Ovington av n Stewart av

CARPENTERS.
Ryker Henry, 72d n 2d av
Volkenburg Von J. 67th c 2d av

CARRIAGE MAKER.
Ulsamer Francis J. 4th av n 65th

CIGAR DEALERS.
Ehlenberger George, Ovington av n Stewart av
Koch William, 3d av n 65th

CLERGYMEN.
Jeffries William E. Ovington av n 4th av
Morgan William H. 67th n 3d av

COAL AND WOOD.
Bennett W. E. & Co.
Wardell W. Bennett. ft Bay Ridge av

DRESSMAKERS.
Braman 3d av n Ovington av
Degroff Fannie, Bay Ridge av n 3d av
Santos Mary A. Bay Ridge av n 3d av
Stilwell Hannah, Bay Ridge av n 3d av
Ulsamer Mary, Stewart av n Cowenhowen la
Van Horn Emma, 3d av n Ovington av

EXPRESS.
O'Connell John, 66th n 1st av

FLORISTS.
Dean James, 3d av & 66th
Ditzenberger Bros. Stewart av n 74th
Keller John M. 66th n 4th av
Molatsch Henry, Bay Ridge av n Franklin av
Weiman Max. Cowenhoven la n Franklin av
Weir Jas. & Sons, 68th c 5th av

FRUIT.
Manley Bros. 4th av c Hegeman's la
Meyer Bros. Ovington av n Stewart av

GROCERS.
Alexander Bros. Ovington av c Stewart
Bennett W. E. (estate of) Bay Ridge av n Shore rd
Cartwright Martha, 66th n 6th av
Laemmel William, Ovington n 4th av
Self & Moore, 3d av c Bay Ridge av
Wardell Elmore H. Bay Ridge av n Shore rd

HAIRDRESSER.
May Wm. H. 3d av n Bay Ridge av

HORSESHOER.
Parker James, Bay Ridge av n 3d av

HOTELS.
Cooney Wm. J. 3d av c Wakeman pl
Koch Hhilip, 3d av c 60th
Lee Alex, 3d av c Bay Ridge av
Warth John, 3d av c 65th

ICE CREAM.
Meyne Charles J. 3d av n Bay Ridge av

LIQUORS.
Benson Thomas, 65th n 4th av
Fette Henry, Bay Ridge av c Shore rd
Koch Willam, 3d av & 65th
Koolwyk P Von De, 3d av cor 65th
Leonhard Philip, 96th n Stewart av
Peisen Gustave, 6th av & 65th
Riehleim George, 65th c 4th av
Robinson & McAvoy, 65th n 4th av
Walsh James, 65th n 4th av

LUMBER DEALERS
Bay Ridge Mfg Co. 66th n 3d av

MILK.
Kohlman Henry C. 66th n 6th av
Laemmel Otta, Ovington av n 4th av
McKeary James, 65th n 6th av

NURSES.
De-Nyse M. L. Bay Ridge av n 3d av
Kiser Mary, Franklin av
Wardell Sally, Bay Ridge av & shore rd

PAINTERS.
Barrett Henry, 3d av n 65th
Lyons William, 66th n 3d av

PLUMBER.
Cook John, 3d av n Bay Ridge av

RESTAURANT.
Degroff Alfred, 3d av & 65th

STRAW HAT MFR
Eames H. A. 2d av n 66th & 594 B'way N. Y.

VARIETIES.
Cartwright Martha, 66th n 6th av
Cook Mary, 3d av n Bay Ridge av
Wakefield Wm. 2d av n Bay Ridge av

REEBER & CO. Second-hand Lumber, Counters, Show Cases, Doors, Window Sashes, Ice Boxes, Shelving, Tin, &c., Bought and Sold. Old Buildings Bought and Removed. 527 to 531 FLUSHING AVE., and 266 LEE AVE., B'KLYN.

"castles" constructed on the property. W. H. Thomas had a mansion built on Second Avenue. Its center hall was wide enough for two teams of horses to ride abreast. Thirteen rooms of that house had to be removed when 75th Street was opened.

In 1848, the original road from Gowanus to Yellow Hook was straightened and widened from 60th Street (the city line) to Van Brunt's Lane (about 79th Street). Later known as Third Avenue, it was lined with elm trees and became the major transportation corridor in the area. Horse cars, and later stagecoaches, were replaced about 1878 with steam engines (dummies) in square cabs which pulled one or two cars. Electric trolleys began service along Third Avenue on May 23, 1892. The village of Bay Ridge was centered at Third Avenue and Pope's Lane (Bay Ridge Avenue).

In 1854, in the 1775 Chandler White house, a meeting between Cyrus Field, Peter Cooper, and others, took place. Papers, which made possible the laying of the first Atlantic cable, were signed. The inaugural message was sent from England on August 16, 1858 by Queen Victoria.

In 1851, William J. Cropsey, eager to (win a bet that he could) evade six weeks' jury duty, joined the famous Kings County Troop. He stayed for 19 years including Civil War service, rising to the rank of colonel, and spending $40 on epaulets alone!

Men from Bay Ridge who were not in active service during the Civil War belonged to the Kings County Troop. They were called upon to quell the draft riots in New York City. David C. Bennett, a tenant farmer on Chandler White's land, had a number of southern blacks in his service who were threatened by the Irish living in the vicinity of Third and Fifth Avenues from 88th to 96th Streets. Bennett hid them in a covered market wagon and drove them into Manhattan. From there he arranged their safe passage to Canada.

Many of the small pre-Civil War houses still standing between 86th Street and the water are remnants of the Irish settlement established around 1850 as a result of the Great Famine in Ireland. Ned Harrigan, successful songwriter and comedian of the team *Harrigan and Hart*, lived there after the Civil War.

In the mid nineteenth century, rich Brooklyn businessmen began building country houses in the Bay Ridge area. From their stately verandas they could view the harbor, while sipping cognac and puffing on fine Cuban "segars." By the 1880s, these capitalists were able to stay in close contact with their factories and offices via a modern technological wonder—the telephone.

After leaving Ovington Village, Henry A. Kent built a magnificent stone mansion just within Brooklyn, at 59th Street between Second and Third Avenues.

On the present site of Owl's Head Park, stood the house of State Senator Henry C. Murphy. Founder of *The Brooklyn Eagle* (1841), and its editor for six years, Senator Murphy, former Minister to Holland, attorney, and local historian, drafted legislation authorizing the construction of the Brooklyn Bridge in 1866. His house, formerly located at Colonial Road and 67th Street, with its driveway on Third Avenue, had owls' heads guarding each gate post. Senator Street is named for him.

Eliphalet W. Bliss, partner of oil magnate Charles Pratt, purchased Murphy's 65-acre estate. Bliss erected a granite observatory tower, whose foundations still exist, overlooking the bay. When Mr. Bliss' widow died in 1905, her will decreed that the estate become a park. The mansion was demolished in the late 1920s, and the land acquired by the Parks Department in 1928. Robert Moses opened the park in 1937.

Conceived in 1870, the New York and Hempstead Rail Road was to run from Bay Ridge to Queens and points eastward. By building a waterfront terminal at Bay Ridge, local farmers anticipated a reduction in freight costs. Headed by investor Abraham Wakeman after the Panic of 1873, the line was reincorporated as the New York, Bay Ridge and Jamaica Railroad. A commuter branch to Coney

Island was added in 1876. Realizing the economic potential of these routes, railroad tycoon Austin Corbin purchased the line from Wakeman in 1876, reorganizing it as the New York and Manhattan Beach Railway Company. Steamboat connections from the railroad's terminus at First Avenue and 65th Street brought passengers to and from Manhattan, Coney Island, Staten Island, and New Jersey. Within a few years, Corbin's Long Island Rail Road absorbed the line, making it its Bay Ridge Division.

Built in 1839, and demolished in 1926, the William R. Bennett homestead stood near the northeast corner of 79th Street and Shore Road. His farm extended back to Third Avenue and is now the site of the block-long Embassy Apartments, built in the late 1920s. Next door, on the south corner of 77th Street, stood the large house of his father, J. Remsen Bennett. Just north of 77th Street, the old home of Van Brunt Bergen survived until the late 1930s. Just south of 79th Street, and extending beyond 80th Street, was Jaques Van Brunt's farm. His house stood in the center of 79th Street on the crest of the hill. Although the original house was demolished, the old kitchen and dining room were moved, and served as garage to a new home at 80th Street. Traveling south, on the westernmost tip of Long Island, was the Daniel Van Brunt house. The property was later inherited by his son Rulef J.

Shortly after the Civil War ended, the Bay Ridge Atheneum was built on the east side of Second Avenue, slightly north of Ovington Avenue. The building's great hall was used for concerts, church fairs and dances, and strawberry festivals. Monthly meetings of the Bay Ridge and Fort Hamilton Citizens' Association took place at the Atheneum. Demolished about 1905, the wood-frame structure was replaced by a row of brick houses which still stand.

About 1880, New Utrecht Town Hall, which included prison cells, was built on 86th Street, Bay Ridge. The Kings County Inebriate Asylum, an imposing turreted building at 90th Street, west of Second Avenue, was erected around that time. It is now the site of the Visitation Academy. A large YMCA was also built at that time.

By 1880, Fort Hamilton had become a fashionable summer resort, featuring no less than a dozen hotels and boardinghouses. They included The Grand View, Otto Hass', The Live Oak, Pope's, Church's, The United States, The Sea View, The Ocean, The Newman House, The Brooklyn House, The Bay View, Connolly's, and others. The original Hamilton House, managed by Hawley D. Clapp, burned down about 1880. A few years later, the Grand View burned while volunteer firemen were holding a ball at Town Hall.

The largest factory in Bay Ridge during the late 1800s belonged to the Eames Straw Hat Company. Located near Second Avenue (now Ridge Boulevard) and 66th Street, H. A. Eames' New York offices were at No. 594 Broadway.

Prior to New Utrecht's 1894 annexation by Brooklyn, 92nd Street was known as Atlantic Avenue, 94th Street was called Washington Avenue, and 95th Street was named Lafayette Street. One Hundredth Street was Denyse Street, and Fourth Avenue was Stewart Avenue, later Hamilton Avenue. Ninety-eighth Street was Clark Street and 96th Street was Church Street. First Avenue became Colonial Road. Narrows Avenue wasn't completely opened until the last estates along Shore Road were broken up, during the 1930s.

After Fourth Avenue was opened and graded in 1869, Rulef Van Brunt planted willow trees which decorated the avenue until subway construction began in 1912.

At Shore Road and 83rd Street stood Isaac Bergen's home. Just to its south, near 84th Street, was Judge Charles Van Brunt's estate. His brother, John Holmes Van Brunt, built a newer house which stood until the 1930s.

Bay Ridge and the Van Brunts made the front pages of the country's newspapers on December 14, 1874 and for several days thereafter. At two o'clock in the morning, John Holmes Van Brunt, who was ill in his house at Shore Road, across from where the Fort Hamilton High school now stands, heard a burglar alarm and the slamming of a shutter in the house next door. It was the home of his brother, Judge Charles C. Van Brunt, 200 yards away, and temporarily unoccupied. He called his son, Albert, to investigate.

Albert saw a light in the upstairs bedroom, heard voices, and hid as two men passed close. He ran home, rousing the estate superintendent and several hired men, who surrounded the house. In a short time two men came out a back door. Holmes Van Brunt, from his sick bed, challenged, "Who goes there?" in a voice that could be heard blocks away. The men fired a shot and ran back inside. Ten minutes later they attempted to dash for a hedge. Holmes told Albert to let them have it. One of the intruders fell and the other dropped but raised up and attempted to draw his pistol. He was felled

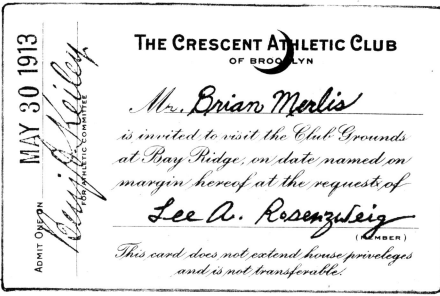

⇒ The names have been changed to protect the innocent....

by a shotgun butt. Holmes Van Brunt demanded, "Who are you?" The intruder gave his name as Joe Douglas, said his companion was William Mosher, and confessed, "We stole Charlie Ross!"

The Charlie Ross kidnaping was as electrifying in its day as the Lindbergh case of the 1930s. Five months before the Bay Ridge incident, brothers Walter and Charlie Ross, aged six and four, while playing in the front yard of their home in the Philadelphia suburb of Germantown, had been abducted by a couple of men in a buggy. Walter was found alive eight miles away in Kensington, but Charlie was still missing.

Toward morning Holmes Van Brunt told Douglas, "You're going to die; you'd better tell us where the child is." Douglas answered, "Mosher knows." He admitted they had tried to enter the Daniel Van Brunt home but had been frightened by the barking of a dog. Then Douglas died. Christian K. Ross brought Walter to New York to view the bodies of the two men. Walter readily identified them as the men who had taken him and Charlie for a buggy ride, one of them had a crooked finger. This was verified. Mosher's brother-in-law, a dismissed New York policeman named Westervelt, was convicted as an accomplice, and served seven years in solitary confinement, but Charlie Ross was never found.

The rowboat used by Mosher and Douglas would later be tied up at Bergen's dock at 83rd Street, and occasionally used by the neighborhood children. Many years later, during demolition of Rulef Van Brunt's house, remnants of the rowboat were discovered under the porch.

Judge Charles Van Brunt's old homestead was demolished in 1890 when the Crescent Athletic Club, in partnership with the Nereid Boat Club, purchased the Van Brunt and Bergen estates. The Crescent Club was established in 1884 as a collegiate football club based in Park Slope. The club built a golf course, extending from 77th to 88th Streets between Colonial and Shore Roads, beside Rulef Van Brunt's home. When the clubhouse was completed in 1892, it quickly became a center of Brooklyn's social life. Its glass-enclosed dining room overlooking the bay, and its great veranda which hugged Shore Road, attracted Brooklyn's social elite.

The Crescent's football team was the American Football Union's national champions for years, shutting out its opponents for three consecutive seasons. Their 1899 baseball team finished second in the Amateur League. In international tennis, the club's grass courts were the predecessors of Forest Hills Stadium. A magnificent boathouse on the water quickly became a mecca for yachtsmen. For years, world-class lacrosse teams attracted crowds to Bay Ridge every Saturday through spring. The championship was held every Decoration Day.

The world's greatest tennis players competed there. Dwight Davis, donor of the Davis Cup, played doubles with Holcombe Ward at the Crescent. The first Davis Cup match was played there in 1902 with President Theodore Roosevelt among the nearly 14,000 spectators. Aviators Wilbur and Orville Wright engaged in matches there. In 1912, President Taft reviewed the Anniversary Day Parade as the Bay Ridge Division marched on the Crescent Club grounds.

In 1931, the Crescent Athletic Club moved to Huntington, Long Island. It has been reported that the boathouse burned down about 1930 in a spectacular fire.

At 83rd Street and Ridge Boulevard stood the Bullock House. Occupied in later years by William L. Dowling, the house overlooked the bay. An informal Sunday School, organized by Mrs. Dowling, led to plans which formed the Bay Ridge Presbyterian Church. After Dowling demolished the house, he subdivided the property lying between 83rd and 85th Streets, Third Avenue and Colonial Road.

The James P. Farrell House was built about 1840 at Shore Road and 95th Street. Wool merchant James P. Farrell raised four children in the house and died in 1910. Two years later, Francis C. Feldmann purchased the property about the time the house was moved 100 feet inland. The Feldmanns occupied the house until the 1970s.

Due to the efforts of community activists, the Landmarks Preservation Commission designated the Bennet-Farrell-Feldmann House as a landmark in 1999. This action ensured the survival of one of Brooklyn's last free-standing Greek Revival homes.

The Bay Ridge Improvement Company was incorporated in November 1890. Its president was Daniel Lewis, also president of the Brooklyn City Railroad Company. The company bought half a million dollars of farmland in New Utrecht Township, and soon offered for sale 3,000 building lots located between Eighth and Fourteenth Avenues, and 69th and 86th Streets. Land purchased from farmers for $1,500 per acre in 1890 was sold two years later for nearly $1,000 per lot!

Sutler on Fort Lafayette - ca. 1870

This store sold merchandise to servicemen on the small island.

In 1894 the Town of New Utrecht was annexed to the City of Brooklyn, becoming its 30th Ward.

On September 28, 1899, a flagpole was erected by the citizens and school children of Bay Ridge and Fort Hamilton to honor Admiral Dewey, hero of the U.S. defeat of the Spanish fleet at Manila Bay.

George Appels' Golden Horn Fort Hamilton Brewery opened prior to 1900 on the east side of Third Avenue between 96th and 97th Streets.

The Bay Ridge Reading Club formed a free library in 1880 in the Atheneum. Within a few years, the club built a small library near today's branch. In 1901, the building and its 6,000-book collection were incorporated into the Brooklyn Public Library, becoming its Bay Ridge Branch. The old building was demolished in 1958 and a new library opened in 1960 at No. 7223 Ridge Boulevard.

In the late 1890s, Mrs. Gelston of Shore Road donated a small collection of books to the community. Known as the Fort Hamilton Free Library, the Brooklyn Public Library adopted the collection in 1901. Andrew Carnegie's $1.6 million gift financed construction of the present Fort Hamilton Branch at No. 9424 Fourth Avenue, designed by Lord and Hewlett, and completed in 1906.

The McKinley Park Branch began as a deposit station at Fort Hamilton Parkway and 70th Street in 1911. The current library was opened in 1959 and renovated in 1995. The Dyker Branch opened in 1974, and has recently undergone an extensive renovation.

In 1900, Public School No. 102, at Ridge Boulevard from 71st to 72nd Street, replaced a little red-frame schoolhouse built about 1883 in the Queen Anne style. Previously known as Bay Ridge District School No. 2. Prior to this, a small yellow schoolhouse stood at 73rd Street and Third Avenue on land donated by Jaques Van Brunt, Sr. Only the best students could advance to Erasmus Hall in Flatbush.

During the late 1800s, the Robinson Estate was built on Shore Road near 93rd Street. Actress Lillian Russell moved there in the 1920s and lived there until her beau, Diamond Jim Brady, purchased the Johnson House, built in 1895 by the McNally Brothers at Shore Road and 99th Street. The Johnsons' son, Tom L., became the three-term three-cent-fare mayor of Cleveland, Ohio. During Prohibition, the house, also known as the Shell House for its roof tiles imported from Italy, became a speakeasy and casino. Lillian Russell moved in during the 1920s. After the 1937 sale to the Sisters of St. Joseph, the structure became Fontbonne Hall Academy, named in honor of Mother St. John Fontbonne, a religious leader during the French Revolution. The school opened in 1939 with forty students. Enlarged over the years, Fontbonne continues to serve as a Catholic college preparatory academy for young women.

Established in Downtown Brooklyn in 1854, the Polytechnic Preparatory Country Day School moved to its current 25-acre campus at 92nd Street and Seventh Avenue in 1917. Known to most as Poly Prep, it was one of the nation's first co-educational private secondary schools to adopt the model of a country day school—offering a well-balanced curriculum and encouraging shared parental responsibility.

Victory Memorial Hospital traces its origins back to the Bay Ridge Hospital, Dispensary and Training School for Nurses, established in 1889 and incorporated in 1904. The original infirmary was located at Second Avenue and 60th Street. After World War I, a new building was completed at the northwest corner of Seventh Avenue and 92nd Street. The hospital changed its name to Victory Memorial Hospital and Skilled Nursing Center.

Although Methodist services were held in the town as early as 1822, it was not until 1830 that a Church was built at Conover's Lane and Sixth Avenue.

The St. John's Episcopal Church cornerstone was laid in 1835, although the roots of this denomination go back to the early Federal period. Two Denyse daughters married former British officers who had both been influential in the organization of The English Episcopal movement.

Christ Church Episcopal was established in 1851 by several prominent Brooklyn families who spent the summer months in Yellow Hook. A church was built at Third Avenue and 68th Street, and on May 22, 1854, Dr. John Seeley Stone officiated the first service. In attendance were members of the Ovington Village Association, who felt that St. John's Episcopal was too far. A Sunday school was established in 1877. With money bequeathed by Eliphalet W. Bliss, the congregation purchased property at Bay Ridge

Bay Ridge Atheneum - east side of Second Avenue north of Ovington Avenue - ca. 1880

Photographed stereoscopically on glass by George Brainard, this structure was built about 1870. The Bay Ridge Post Office, supervised by William Wakefield, was located here along with his variety store. Dr. Myers' office was upstairs. The Bay Ridge Brass Band, led by J. F. Hernandez, rehearsed and performed at the Atheneum. Row houses have occupied this site since about 1905.

Boulevard and 73rd Street, where a cornerstone was laid on November 1, 1908. The first service in the current structure was conducted on Easter, March 27, 1910.

Holding its first service on April 29, 1906 at Firemen's Hall, (257 Bay Ridge Avenue), the congregation, soon to be known as the Church of the Good Shepherd, was formed. Three years later, they purchased the vacant Christ Church Episcopal. The church was moved to its current location at Fourth Avenue and 75th Street, with services reconvening on Easter, March 27, 1910. The building was reconstructed and stuccoed during the 1960s.

St. Patrick's Roman Catholic Church is the area's oldest Catholic Church. Predating the formation of the Diocese of Brooklyn, its first mass was celebrated in 1843 in Cummin's barn (Shore Road and 99th Street).

Our Lady of Perpetual Help Roman Catholic Church was established in 1894. The massive shrine, Brooklyn's largest church, was constructed near 59th Street and Fifth Avenue during the early 1900s.

In 1918, The Union Church of Bay Ridge was created by the joining of Bay Ridge Presbyterian and Bay Ridge Dutch Reformed Churches, both formed in 1896.

Bay Ridge Jewish Center was established and built in the 1920s as a Conservative congregation. Its unique curved entrance can still be seen on the northeast corner of Fourth Avenue and 81st Street.

In 1950, Trinity Lutheran Church and St. Mary's Greek Orthodox Church built edifices in Bay Ridge. In recent years, mosques and temples have been established in the area as houses of worship for Muslims and Asians. A Kingdom Hall was built by the Bible & Tract Society for the area's Jehovah Witnesses.

Neighborhood residents take great pride in their valiant wartime service. During World War I, the shore from 69th to 86th Streets was lined with dozens of rows of gray barracks. The Bennett house at the foot of 79th Street was used as a canteen. A block south, at 80th Street, the Jaques Van Brunt home was used as a hostess house where wives, sweethearts, and sisters of the soldiers congregated on the home's wide veranda and in its spacious rooms. The Chandler White, Van Brunt Bergen, and Church residences were all called into service for convalescent soldiers or hostess houses.

An unusual house has stood at No. 8220 Narrows Avenue at 82nd Street since 1917. Designed by J. Sarsfield Kennedy for shipping magnate Howard E. Jones, the house is built of boulders. Known as The Gingerbread House or the Hansel and Gretel House, it has been a New York City landmark since 1988.

The Dover Patrol Monument, a granite obelisk designed by Sir Aston Webb, was erected in 1931 and placed at the west end of Fort Hamilton Park. The monument honors participation of the United States Navy in World War I. Identical monuments stand in Dover, England, and in Cap Blanc Nez, France. The monument was moved for the placement of the Brooklyn anchorage of the Verrazano-Narrows Bridge.

Although nearly all construction projects ceased during World War I, the Fourth Avenue subway reached Bay Ridge in 1916. It was not until the 1920s that Bay Ridge and Fort Hamilton felt the results of this improvement. During that decade, blocks of row houses quickly sprang up while apartment houses rose on Fourth Avenue, Shore Road, and Ridge Boulevard. The population of Bay Ridge doubled between 1910 and 1924. By the end of the decade, Bay Ridge had become urbanized, absorbing a new cosmopolitan population. Schools, churches, stores, cinemas, and public facilities were established or enlarged to provide for the new residents. A local paper, *The Brooklyn Spectator*, was established in 1933. *The Home Reporter and Sunset News* has been a favorite of the locals since 1953.

Hotel Gregory, located at No. 8315 Fourth Avenue since the 1920s, became part of the Comfort Inn chain about 1990 after extensive renovation.

By the 1940s, tens of thousands of Bay Ridge residents could proudly trace their ancestry to the Scandinavian countries of Norway, Sweden, and Finland. The neighborhood also boasted a considerable number of Italians, Sicilians, Greeks, Irish, and Germans. The area has experienced a recent influx of Asians, Middle Easterners, Russians, Indians, and Pakistanis. Since the 1970s, the Spanish tongue has replaced Finnish and Norwegian in the northern part of the community, toward Sunset Park.

Dummy Engine No. 7 at Fort Hamilton - 1885

The *Bay View* was a steam powered dummy. It was owned and operated by the Brooklyn City Rail Road Company. Passengers were taken from Fort Hamilton to Hamilton Ferry in Red Hook by Third and Hamilton Avenues. From there, a ferry would take them to the Battery. This photograph was taken near the foot of Fort Hamilton Avenue (Parkway), next to the army base.

The area has always offered fine dining, dancing and entertainment to residents and visitors alike. The Merlis' Shore Road Casino was popular after World War II until the 1950s. The Harbor House and The Hamilton House were landmarks during the 1960s. The dance scenes from the 1977 movie *Saturday Night Fever* were filmed at the disco 2001 Space Odyssey, now Prism, on Eighth Avenue. Other popular clubs/bars during the '70s' disco craze were Horsefeathers, Mustard Seed, Pastels, Brown Derby, Yesterdays, Nell Flaherty's, Chelsea Station, and The Brooklyn Dodger. Today's popular restaurants include Embers, Gazebo, Devines, Club Rio, Skinflints, T J Bentley's, Pipins, 101, Dario's, Griswold's Pub, Short Ribs, Salty Dog, Casa Pepe, New Corner, Judge & Jury, Peggy O'Neills, Chadwicks, Hunters Steak & Ale House, Lily's Public House, The Wicked Monk, da Tommaso, Ballybunion, Limestones, and Chianti. The neighborhood also boasts numerous restaurants offering international cuisine.

The neighborhood boasts three annual celebrations. The Third Avenue Festival and The Ragamuffin Parade, both in September, and the Norwegian Constitution Day Parade, held in May since 1951.

On September 9, 1991, a gas explosion at No. 333 86th Street killed three and injured twenty-seven residents.

Plans to link Brooklyn to Staten Island began in the years following World War I. A projected tunnel from Owl's Head Park was actually commenced in 1921 under Mayor John Hylan. A shaft between Shore Road and the Belt Parkway, at the foot of 68th Street, still exists. The abandoned project was referred to as Hylan's Folly.

The idea of a bridge was vetoed in 1936 by the War Department. It was felt that linking the boroughs would present a threat to national security.

In 1949, after public hearings before a joint military board, the Federal Government granted the Triborough Bridge and Tunnel Authority a permit to construct a bridge. Although 82 civic groups fought hard to prevent the eventual displacement of 2,500 families, the proponents of the project, led by Robert Moses, claimed victory in Albany. Work began in April 1959, and traffic opened on the upper roadway on November 1, 1964, a year ahead of schedule. Ferry service was discontinued on November 25.

The Verrazano-Narrows Bridge was engineered by Othmar Ammann, the world's foremost bridge builder.

Ammann, senior partner of the firm of Ammann & Whitney, an octogenarian during this project, having come to America from Switzerland in 1904. He had worked on The Golden Gate Bridge, and designed the George Washington, Triborough, Throgs Neck, Bronx-Whitestone, Goethals, and Bayonne Bridges. He also designed The Outerbridge Crossing.

The Verrazano-Narrows was the world's longest suspension bridge, spanning 4,260 feet between the 690-foot-high towers. The foundation of the Brooklyn tower rests upon the remains of Fort Lafayette. About 143,000 miles of wire suspends the weight of twelve traffic lanes—six on each level. Over 600,000 cubic yards of concrete were used in the course of constructing the 13,700-foot-long engineering marvel. The entire project, including construction, administration, and financing, cost 305 million dollars.

Although not initially embraced by local residents, this magnificent bridge, linking the boroughs of Brooklyn and Staten Island, is revered by the community as a symbol of unity, and a monument to local pride.

Bay Ridge-Fort Hamilton, Brooklyn's most culturally diverse neighborhood, has proven its fortitude by adapting to change—both internal and external. As this beautiful district proudly enters the twenty-first century, its residents proudly recall the area's rich and colorful heritage.

Children bathing off Fort Hamilton - Fort Lafayette in the background - 1907

Fort Lafayette - 1895

Fort Hamilton Parkway and Ninety-ninth Street - 1895

Built by soldiers from the nearby garrison on land donated by the Denyse family, St. John's Church was known as the Church of the Generals. Among its parishioners were Robert E. Lee, Thomas "Stonewall" Jackson, and Abner Doubleday. Lee, who sponsored Jackson's baptism, served as vestryman from 1842 to 1844. The old church survived until 1897. On Ninety-ninth Street, next to the entrance to the new church, a tree planted by Robert E. Lee still stands.

Strolling In Fort Hamilton - 1895

The Simon Cortelyou Homestead - ca. 1895

This ancient landmark with a gambrel roof faced the Road to Denyse's Ferry, near where Seventh Avenue would reach the bay, within the present confines of Fort Hamilton Reservation. The stone house was built by laborers sent by Governor Peter Stuyvesant to replace the original Cortelyou House, destroyed by fire in 1675. When Pieter Cortelyou died in 1757, his son Simon, followed by his grandson, Simon Jr., occupied the homestead. William Post purchased the property in 1836. The Federal Government, desiring to enlarge Fort Hamilton, acquired title to it in 1892. The landmark was demolished in 1894 amid profound sorrow by Government officials. The sum of $1,000 would have saved the house. During the American Revolution, British General Howe slept in the house after his August 1776 landing at New Utrecht.

Bathhouses along the Beach at Bay Ridge - 1900

Unique construction on West side of Third Avenue, between 83rd and 84th Sts. Double apartments over two stores at each end of the block, with six two-family buildings in the centre. Purchasers for practically all of these are waiting for their completion.

Our Brooklyn Office, Southwest corner Third Avenue and 73rd St.

1905

Two brick-and-stone blocks under construction on East side of Third Avenue at 77th and 78th Streets. Upper block is seen in distance in lower view. These stores and apartments were nearly all rented, and several of the buildings sold, at this stage of construction and in mid-winter.

Bay Ridge Branch of the Manual Training High School, 71st St. near Second Avenue.
Public School No. 102, at Second Avenue and 71st St.   Public School No. 127, Seventh Avenue, 78th and 79th Sts.

20-Inch Rodman Gun At Fort Hamilton

One of the two produced, this cannon, weighing 116,000 pounds, was designed by Captain Thomas Jefferson Rodman and was the largest cannon ever built until that time. The gun was expected to send a half-ton cannonball a distance of 5 miles. The first shot did not even reach the water, and the gun jammed during its second trial. A man had to crawl in the 20-inch bore to clear the obstruction. Although the second shot traveled a distance into the bay, the gun's military effectiveness was judged to be minimal, and the weapon was moved to John Paul Jones Park.

Bliss Estate, as seen from Shore Road - 1906

E. W. Bliss was born at Cooperstown, New York in 1836. By age 23 he managed the Charles Parker Gun Company of Meriden, Connecticut. After seeing action at Bull Run during the Civil War, he linked up with Charles Pratt and Frederick W. Devoe, who were prominent Brooklynites in the oil industry. Bliss moved to Brooklyn in 1866, where he invented and secured patents for torpedoes and other projectiles. He purchased the Henry C. Murphy estate with additional lands totaling sixty-five acres, at Bay Ridge. Bliss erected an observatory tower of granite at a cost of $16,000. Although the tower and mansion are gone today, part of the property is preserved as Owl's Head Park, which became public in the 1920s.

NIELS POULSON RESIDENCE, Bay Ridge. Interior View.

A magnificent interior of metal, designed and made by Mr. Poulson, to whom is due much credit for the modern advance in structural-metal adornment, in residential, business, and ornamental structures. Mr. Poulson is President of the Hecla Iron Works.

from King's Views - 1905

Neil Poulson's Residence - Shore Road near Eighty-ninth Street - 1907

Constructed with steel frames and an all-copper exterior, this mansion was the first fireproof house.

Sea Gate, Coney Island, in distance — Photo. by Enrique Muller

FORT HAMILTON PARK, Shore Road and Fort Hamilton Parkway. One of Brooklyn's four seaside-parks.

At southern end of Fort Hamilton Parkway, Shore Road Junction, facing the Lower Bay. Seven acres. Popular summer-resort near the United States Government reservation and harbor defences. Opposite Fort Lafayette. Beautiful view of the harbor, from Coney Island and Sandy Hook to the Narrows.

from King's Views - 1905

Steam Ferryboat *Bay Ridge* - 1907

Horse-drawn trucks loaded with merchandise will be the first to disembark. Ferry service from Bay Ridge terminated on November 25, 1964.

Teutonia Gesang Verein **(German Singing Society) of Fort Hamilton - ca. 1908**

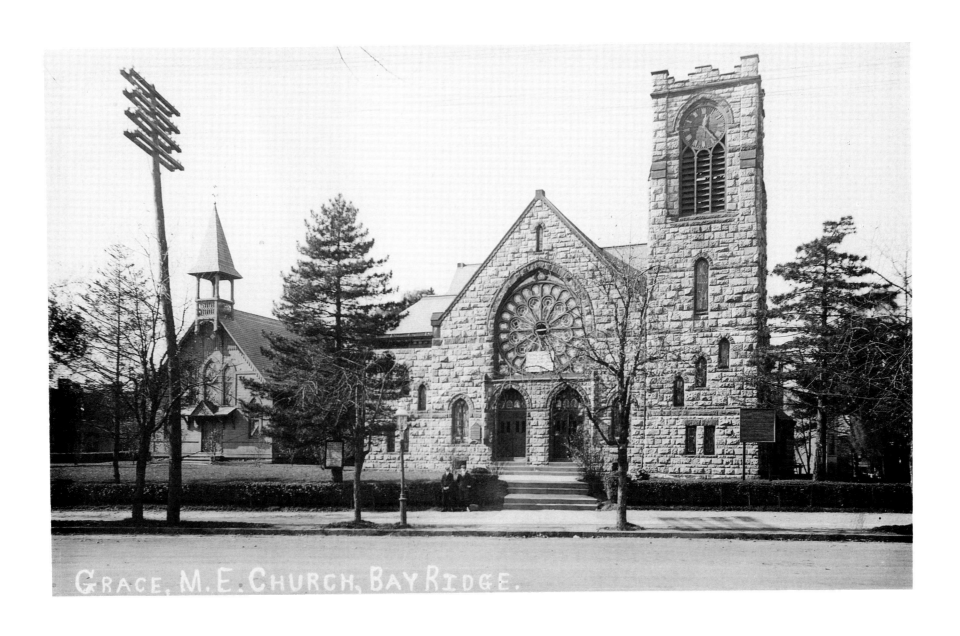

Grace Bay Ridge Methodist Episcopal Church, established 1830 - southwest corner Fourth and Ovington Avenues - 1908

The wooden chapel at the left was replaced by Our Savior's Norwegian Lutheran Church during the 1920s.

Bay Cliff Villa - 1909

This residence belonged to Mary C. Broome and was located 100 feet east of Shore Road, between Ninety-third and Oliver Streets. It faced the bay.

Eighty-eighth Street east from First Avenue (Colonial Road) to Ridge Boulevard - 1909

A full-color reproduction of this post card is featured on the back cover.

Norwegian Lutheran Deaconesses' Home & Hospital Ambulance - 1910

This horse-drawn ambulance transported the injured and infirm. The Norwegian Lutheran Deaconesses' Home and hospital, located at Fourth Avenue at Fourty-sixth Street, was established in 1883. It cared for all persons, except those with contagious diseases. The hospital offered its services at no charge to the poor. This hospital was the predecessor of today's Lutheran Medical Center.

Road leading to the bay from Shore Road at Ninety-seventh Street - 1910

Shore Road northwest at Ninety-seventh Street - 1910

A junk dealer pushes his wares uphill. At Ninety-fifth Street the old Bennett homestead is visible just to the left of the gas lamp.

Fifth Avenue northeast from Fifty-seventh Street - 1910

As Fifth Avenue exits Bay Ridge, it will continue through Sunset Park, border Green-Wood Cemetery, enter Park Slope, cross Flatbush Avenue, and end at Atlantic Avenue. This view is looking toward Fifty-sixth Street. Northbound open-air trolley No. 603 originated at Coney Island, and is headed toward the Thirty-ninth Street Ferry. Rubbers are offered for sale at the store on the left.

Fort Hamilton Station - Brooklyn Post Office - Nos. 7914-7918 Third Avenue - ca. 1910

Post Office employees proudly pose for photographer J. L. Manney. The Post Office later moved to Fourth Avenue and remained there until a new building was built about 1980 at No. 8801 Fifth Avenue. Fort Hamilton's zip code is 11209.

Bay Ridge Park showing elevated railroad on Third Avenue - 1912

The smokestacks at the left belonged to the Brooklyn Edison Company. The Fifth Avenue elevated turned at Thirty-eighth Street and continued along Third Avenue, terminating at Sixty-fifth Street. This photo was taken from near Sixty-seventh Street, west of Bay Ridge High School.

Shore Road north from Seventy-fifth Street - 1912

Two Bennett mansions overlook the bay.

Eighty-seventh Street west to Narrows Avenue - 1912

Staten Island is visible beyond New York Bay.

Fourth Avenue northeast at Sixty-fifth Street - 1912

A wagon loaded with hay is parked just beyond Sixty-fifth Street.

Eighty-third Street east from Ridge Boulevard - 1912

No. 8301 Ridge Boulevard dominates this photograph.

Weber Mansion - facing Shore Road, north of Ninety-first Street - 1912

Topped with a Spanish-tiled roof, this mansion was home to Shore Road Hospital from about 1920 to 1950.

Seventy-ninth Street west to Ridge Boulevard - 1912

Shore Road at Seventy-ninth Street, from the Bay - 1912

Seventy-ninth Street was known as Van Brunt's Lane. The Barkaloo and Van Brunt mansions overlook the harbor.

No. 6735 Fourth Avenue - 1912

This apartment house stands just north of the Bay Ridge Baptist Church. Senator Street is at the far left.

Unidentified Women's Club Luncheon at Bay Ridge - 1912

Crescent Athletic Club - Shore Road between Eighty-fourth and Eighty-fifth Streets - 1912

This wooden building was erected in 1891 on land formerly belonging to Charles van Brunt and Isaac Bergen. In 1931 the club sold its property to the city and moved to Huntington, Long Island. Fort Hamilton High School occupies this site today.

75th. Street East from 4th. Avenue, Bay Ridge, 1912 Brooklyn, N.Y.

75th. Street West from 3rd. Avenue, Bay Ridge, 1912 Brooklyn, N. Y.

No. 7618 Fourth Avenue, northwest corner Seventy-seventh Street - 1913

Nos. 7716 and 7718 Fourth Avenue - 1913

Seventy-ninth Street west to Colonial Road - 1913

A single-track railroad, nearly a mile long, was installed along Seventy-ninth Street from Fourth Avenue to the waterfront. Lasting only a year or two, it carried excavated earth from the construction of the Fourth Avenue B.M.T. subway. The earth was used as landfill, forever changing Bay Ridge's coastal profile.

T. J. Farrell's West End Moving Van - 1913

Fourth Avenue in the Seventies.

Seventy-ninth Street west at Narrows Avenue - 1913

Narrows Avenue had not yet been opened to Eightieth Street. A large sailboat is visible on the bay.

Bay Ridge shore, north from Seventy-eighth Street and Shore Road - 1913

Railroad cars litter the beach. Mansions along Shore Road, as well as Manhattan's office buildings are shrouded by an ominously threatening cloud cover.

Seventy-fourth Street west from Third Avenue - 1913

In the distance, at Ridge Boulevard, are a group of twelve two-hundred year-old beech trees known as The Twelve Apostles. They were removed in 1927 when the Townsend home, once known as the William Thomas place, was demolished.

The Electra Theater - northwest corner Third Avenue and Seventy-fifth Street - 1913

The Electra was Bay Ridge's first large motion picture theater. View is west along Seventy-fifth Street. The building, severely altered, now houses a supermarket.

Eighty-fourth Street west from Third Avenue - 1913

Bay Ridge Avenue west from Third Avenue - 1913

Edward Wolff's pharmacy was on the corner at left. On the right corner was Ye Olde Tavern.

Ridge Club - No. 167 Seventy-second Street - 1913

This venerable landmark was demolished about 1935.

Boat House of the Crescent Athletic Club - 1913

Located on the water at Eighty-third Street, this imposing wood-frame building burned down in the 1930s.

Third Avenue north to Seventy-ninth Street - 1913

The corner tavern on the far right offered lamb stew. Just past Seventy-ninth Street is the real estate office of Cornelius B. Van Brunt, a descendant of an old-line New Utrecht family. L. Horowitz's tailor shop is on the left just past Seventy-eighth Street. Note the old-fashioned gas lamp which illuminated the street sign at night.

Eighty-seventh Street west from Third Avenue - 1913

Seventy-ninth Street west to Third Avenue - 1914

The billboard on the right advertises fine cottages with parquet floors from $5,000 to $6,500.

Sleighing Down Seventy-fifth Street Hill - 1914

The children have reached the base of the hill near Colonial road. The mansion was located at No. 151 Seventy-fifth Street. You're looking northeast.

Seventy-ninth Street west to Ridge Boulevard - 1914

No. 7904 Ridge Boulevard is visible to the left.

Fourth Avenue south from Eighty-first Street - 1914

Fourth Avenue north from Seventy-fifth Street - 1915

At the far left, partially visible, is Good Shepherd Lutheran Church. Just past Seventy-fourth Street is Our Lady of Angels Roman Catholic Church. Between Seventy-second Street and Ovington Avenue are Our Saviors Norwegian Lutheran Church and Bay Ridge Methodist Episcopal Church.

West side of Fourth Avenue, north from Seventy-seventh Street - 1915

A woman pushes a baby stroller toward Seventy-sixth Street. Good Shepherd Lutheran Church is visible just past Seventy-fifth Street.

The original Public School No. 104
northeast corner Fifth Avenue and Ninety-second Street - ca. 1915

In 1881, Augustus H. Ely, Henry P. Lugar, and Joshua C. Sanders, trustees of School District No. 4, Town of New Utrecht, had this school erected on land granted to them. Later known as P.S. 104 as well as the Fort Hamilton Elementary School, a brick structure was built behind it in 1907. The wooden structure housed annexes of Erasmus and Bay Ridge High Schools. The building was demolished prior to the 1928 addition to the existing brick schoolhouse.

Bay Ridge Building, Northwest Corner of 72nd Street and Third Avenue, Brooklyn, N. Y. — 1915

Seventy-ninth Street southeast from Thirteenth to Fourteenth Aves., Dyker Heights - 1916

Fourth Avenue north from Seventy-seventh Street - 1916

New Fourth Avenue B.M.T. subway entrance.

Tenth Avenue northeast from Sixty-ninth Street - 1916

The first house, at the corner of Bay Ridge Avenue, is No. 6822 Tenth Avenue.

FORMER PRESIDENT ROOSEVELT. WITH THE CELEBRATED 15TH REGT. BAND, U. S. A. BAND MASTER RESTA ON HIS LEFT.
FORT HAMILTON. 1917 BROOKLYN, N. Y.

Johnson House alias General Stanton House
Northwest corner of Shore Road and 99th Street - 1922

99th Street would be cut through just to the right of the house on the right.

Nos. 8803 - 8809 Fourth Avenue - 1923

The pre-Civil War house (No. 8803 - 8805) would be demolished about 1925. Forest Place, an old road, passed behind these two frame structures.

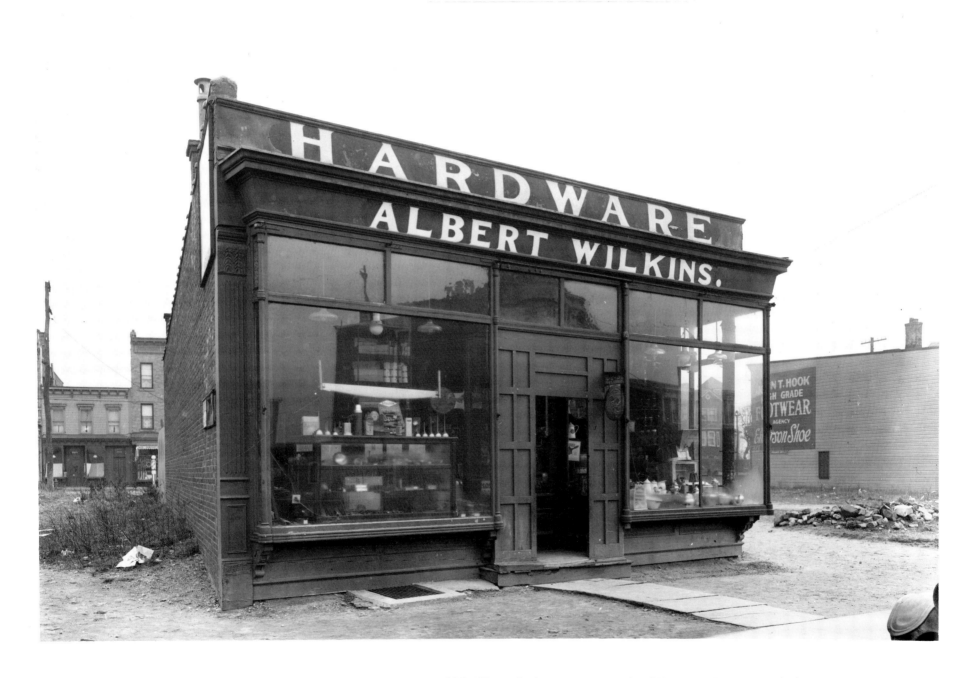

Albert Wilkins' Hardware Store - No. 9227 Fourth Avenue, opposite Ninety-third St. - 1923

Nos. 8622 - 8602 Fourth Avenue - 1923

Eighty-seventh Street is at the far left. These recently constructed buildings will soon be occupied. (Detail at right, corner Eighty-sixth Street.)

Nos. 9313 - 9315 Fourth Avenue - 1923

Two days after Christmas, wreaths still hang in the upstairs windows. An advertisement for the *Home Talk*, a local newspaper, is painted on the side of the building. At the far right is the rear of No. 9240 Fifth Avenue, built in 1888.

Nos. 8819 - 8821 Fourth Avenue, southeast corner Eighty-ninth Street - 1923

The store at left was home to The Bay Ridge Motorcycle Club. Note the porcelain "Fourth Ave." sign on the building's corner.

Confluence of Fourth and Fifth Avenues, north from Ninety-fifth Street - 1923

A patriotic memorial monument and plaque still occupy this triangular parcel.

Shore Road Pharmacy - No. 8727 Fourth Avenue, northeast corner Eighty-eighth St. - 1923

Corrao's Service Station - No. 8917 Fourth Avenue, northeast corner Ninetieth St. - 1923

Corrao sold Socony gasoline for nineteen cents per gallon.

Jack's Gas Station and Auto Supply Store - No. 9109 Fourth Avenue - 1923

Note the two primitive gas pumps resting on the sidewalk.

No. 9318 Fourth Avenue - 1923

Washington Democratic Club - No. 9004 Fourth Ave., southwest corner Ninetieth St. - 1923

Storefronts at No. 9306 Fourth Avenue - 1923

Maguire's Stationery (left) and a real estate office shared the ground floor. Subway-related construction has exposed the building's foundation.

Tom Caruso's Barber Shop - No. 9013 Fourth Avenue - 1923

Fort Hamilton Shoe Repairing and Hat Cleaning Store - 1925

No. 9427 Fifth Avenue, opposite Ninety-fifth Street, at Fourth Avenue.

Fourth Avenue north to Ninety-second Street - 1925

A large six-story apartment house would soon be built on the northwest corner, at left.

Playing bocce on the grounds of the Crescent Athletic Club - 1925

Tennis Tournament on the Crescent Athletic Club's Grass Courts - 1920s

J. Medanes' Gas Station - northwest corner Ninety-second Street and Gatling Place - 1929

**147 85th STREET
BROOKLYN, NEW YORK**

One of the most beautiful homes in Bay Ridge is offered for sale at $20,000.

Here is a home built on a plot of ground 92' by 100' containing 10 rooms, 3 baths, and a two car garage in the finest residential section of Brooklyn. For particulars and inspection see

JOHN B. SWIFT, Agent
471 86th Street   Shore Road 5-0700
Brooklyn, N. Y.

Bay Ridge Real Estate Listings - ca. 1930

**Northwest Corner
Ridge Boulevard and 85th Street
Bay Ridge   Brooklyn**

This beautiful example of Dutch Colonial architecture is offered for sale at $25,000.

This magnificent home built on a plot of ground 100x150 has 12 rooms —4 baths, 2 car garage, nicely landscaped. There is a recreation room in the form of a ship's bridge on the top floor.

For particulars and inspection call

JOHN B. SWIFT, Agent
471 86th Street   SHore Road 5-0700
Brooklyn 9, N. Y.

Fort Hamilton Parkway between One Hundredth and One Hundred First Streets - 1931

Colonel James C. Church built this homestead in 1833. The Fort Hamilton Post Office was located in his general store, at the foot of the road. He also started a stage route from Fort Hamilton to Fulton Ferry, through New Utrecht and Flatbush via the old Kings Highway. In 1844, he began stagecoach service via the Gowanus Road to Hamilton Ferry, a route taken over by the Brooklyn City Rail Road Company, and then the Third Avenue-Hamilton Avenue trolley line. For six years, Church was Colonel of the National Guard Regiment of Brooklyn. Church knew Captain Robert E. Lee and Stonewall Jackson quite well. The house also served as a hotel—Robert E. Lee being its most famous guest. Colonel Church died in 1856. The homestead stood until about 1940.

N.R.A. Parade in Bay Ridge - October 12, 1933

The blue eagle, symbol of the National Recovery Act, marches along Fourth Avenue. Dentist Reuben Kagel peers out his window, just to the right of the eagle's head, at No. 8519 Fourth Avenue.

Barkaloo Cemetery - Narrows Avenue and MacKay Place - 1935

This historic cemetery was established in 1725 by William Harmans Barkaloo, about five hundred feet from his home near Shore Road, where Xaverian High School stands today. Barkaloo is the only remaining homestead cemetery in Brooklyn, and its size (approximately 55 feet by 26 feet) makes it the smallest cemetery in Brooklyn. By 1848, the time of the last burial, the cemetery consisted of about 40 graves. As time went on, and the neighborhood developed, the majority of the graves were moved to their current location and entombed within a concrete vault.

Among those buried here are Harmans Barkaloo, who saw action in the Revolutionary War as well as the French and Indian War. It has been said that he was a personal friend of George Washington. Harmans's brother, Jacques Barkaloo, who saw action in the Battle of Brooklyn also rests here. Jacques was also the first English-speaking teacher in the Town of New Utrecht. The brothers were the sons of William Harmans Barkaloo.

This hallowed ground is also the final resting place of Simon Cortelyou, who was very active in securing guns and ammunition for the Americans to use in the battles of Yorktown, Saratoga, and Brooklyn.

In 1935, an impressive limestone monument was erected by the Veterans of Foreign Wars; Porter Post, to honor the memory of the veterans buried there.

For many years, the cemetery was the victim of vandals, neglect, disrepair, and was used as a garbage dump. In the 1970s and 1980s, a number of repairs and restorations took place, sponsored by The Bay Ridge Historical Society (established in 1976, whose goal is to "preserve and record the history of Bay Ridge for its citizens.)

As we enter the twenty-first century, Barkaloo Cemetery stands as a fitting tribute to those patriots who helped America achieve its independence.

Bay Ridge from the air - 1937

Land is being filled for the Belt Parkway between Fort Hamilton and Owl's Head Park. The small island in the foreground is Fort Lafayette. It would later become the base of the Verrazano-Narrows Bridge's Brooklyn tower.

Fort Hamilton High School - Shore Road at Eighty-third Street - 1941

Situated on the former site of the Crescent Athletic Club house and grounds, this school opened in September 1941 with 2,500 students.

Oliver H. Lund - Real Estate and Insurance Broker - 1940s

Lund's office was at No. 484 Seventy-eighth Street, just west of Fifth Avenue. He and his wife Margaret resided at No. 174 Seventy-third Street.

Brooklyn Dodger Dolph Camilli and family walking near their Bay Ridge home - 1941

Many Dodgers resided in Bay Ridge. "Duke" Snider lived on Colonial Road, "Pee Wee" Reese resided on Ninety-fourth Street between Third and Fourth Avenues. Rube Walker and Wayne Terwilliger shared an apartment on Ninety-fifth Street between Third Avenue and Ridge Boulevard. Married without children at the time, the two couples entertained the Chicago Cubs when they came to town. Andy Pafko taught Sunday School at Trinity Lutheran Church on Third Avenue and Ninety-first Street. Former Met coach and Brooklyn Dodger Joe Pignatano still resides in the area.

Third Avenue northeast from Sixty-seventh Street - 1944

Trolley No. 2576 will turn south on 86th Street, one mile behind the photographer. The approach to the recently constructed Gowanus Expressway is just beyond 65th Street. The man at the left has just stumbled out of Curran's Bar & Grill. Note the old-fashioned street lamps and the cobblestone arrangement. The parking lot at the at the left charged twenty-five cents. The trolley is crossing over the bridge above the tracks of the Long Island Rail Road's Bay Ridge Division, currently owned by Amtrak.

Cosgrove's Restaurant - No. 8625 Fourth Avenue at Eighty-seventh Street - 1940s

The Harbor House was located here until recent years.

Fifth Avenue south to Bay Ridge Parkway (Seventy-fifth Street) - 1944

Fifth Avenue north to Senator Street - 1944

Fifth Avenue north from Bay Ridge Parkway (Seventy-fifth Street) - 1945

The Stanley Theater was built in the 1920s as the Colonial Theater.

1946

Fourth Avenue south to Ninety-ninth Street - 1946

Hartman's dining and dancing establishment is on the right. Trolley tracks along Ninety-ninth Street connected those on Third and Fourth Avenues.

Bay Ridge Avenue southeast at Fort Hamilton Parkway - 1946

Fifth Avenue and Eighty-sixth Street, northeast corner - 1946

Northbound trolley No. 8163 is turning onto Fifth Avenue. The old police precinct, completed about 1910, was replaced by a multi-level municipal parking facility about 1975. The Dyker Theater is on the right.

Fifth Avenue north to Bay Ridge Avenue - 1946

West side of Fifth Avenue north from Eighty-sixth Street - 1946

Southbound trolley No. 8295 passed Rosen's furniture and toy store, Reichert's luncheonette, and will soon obscure the photographer's view of Fanny Farmer's corner confectionery.

Fifth Avenue north to Sixty-eighth Street - 1946

East side of Fifth Avenue north from Ninety-fourth Street - 1946

Southbound trolley No. 8256 will terminate at Fourth Avenue and One Hundred First Street, seven blocks south of here. The old wood-frame Victorian homes no longer exist.

Third Avenue south from Bay Ridge Avenue - 1947

Lepaw's Pharmacy - southwest corner Eighth and Bay Ridge Avenues - 1948

This store served local residents for about 50 years. It closed about 1980. A young girl is about to board the trolley.

Bay Ridge Avenue northwest to Eighth Avenue - 1947

ANDRESEN'S FAMOUS CHOCOLATES
6905 - 5th Ave. Brooklyn 9 N.Y.

ca. 1948

Photo by Rudy Larsen

Blizzard of 1948
Bay Ridge Parkway

Fourth Avenue north to Ninety-Ninth Street - 1948

St. Patrick's Church is visible in the distance, beyond Ninety-seventh Street.

Fourth Avenue north from One Hundredth Street - 1949

This photo was taken on February 19th, the last day of service on the Fifth Avenue line.

Fifth Avenue northeast to Sixty-fourth Street - 1949

Bay Ridge Avenue west from Third Avenue - 1949

Fifth Avenue south at Eighty-sixth Street (close-up at right) - 1949

Fifth Avenue northeast from Sixty-ninth Street (Bay Ridge Avenue) - 1949

The Alpine Theater is still in business.

THE MERLIS' SHORE ROAD CASINO
100th St. & 4th Ave., Brooklyn, N. Y.
Adjacent to Belt Parkway. Shore Road 5-9437.
The most popular entertainment place
in Brooklyn

A MINIMUM AMOUNT Per Person
Due to our elaborate floor show, we are compelled to maintain a minimum charge.
$1.00 from Monday through Thurs.
$2.00 Saturday
$1.50 Fridays, Sundays, Holidays and Holiday Eves.
The minimum may be consumed in food or beverage, or both.
THERE IS NO COVER CHARGE

SHORE ROAD CASINO

THE FEDERAL TAX OF 20%
WILL BE ADDED ON YOUR TOTAL CHECK

•

Any Dissatisfaction in Service
Should Be Reported to the
Management

HOSTS — GEORGE & DAVE

DINE and DANCE
WONDERFUL MUSIC

Not Responsible for Personal Property Unless Checked

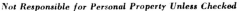

1950

Bay Ridge High School - Fourth Avenue at Sixty-seventh Street - 1951

This all-girls high school originated in an annex to Erasmus Hall High School. The 1915 structure now houses the High School of Telecommunications Art and Technology.

Seventy-second Street west to Ridge Court and Third Avenue - 1957

Gowanus Expressway construction – 1941

?PROGRESS? 1960

Tony's
Caddy
on
Shore
Road

FEB 62

Brooklyn Tower nearing completion, Verrazano-Narrows Bridge - 1962

Bay Ridge, from midway between the Brooklyn Tower and Anchorage, Verrazano-Narrows Bridge - 1963

The approaches and expressway are still under construction. Hamilton House restaurant is visible to the left, facing Fourth Avenue. The Dover Monument is visible among the cluster of trees in John Paul Jones Park.

RKO Dyker Theater - No. 525 Eighty-sixth Street - 1970

This motion picture theater was built in the 1920s. It closed in 1977.

View Along Shore Road - 1970

Hamilton House Restaurant
Fourth Avenue at One Hundred First Street - 1961

Harbor House Restaurant
Fourth Avenue at Eighty-seventh Street - 1970s

Peter's New Royal and Thumann's Luncheonette
Fourth Avenue near Sixty-ninth Street - 1970s

Catalog

WELCOME BACK TO BROOKLYN
by Brian Merlis & Oscar Israelowitz   172 pages
ISBN 1-878741-14-4   **$19.95** Paper (plus $5.00 shipping)

BROOKLYN - THE WAY IT WAS
by Brian Merlis   250 pages   Landscape Format
ISBN 1-878741-52-7   **$29.95**   Hard Cover ($5.00 shipping)

BROOKLYN'S WILLIAMSBURG
City Within A City   by Brian Merlis   240 pages
ISBN 1-878741-66-7   **$39.95**   Hard Cover ($5.00 shipping)

BROOKLYN'S PARK SLOPE - A Photo Retrospective
by Brian Merlis & Lee Rosenzweig
165 pages   Landscape Format
ISBN 1-878741-47-0   **$29.95**   Hard Cover ($5.00 shipping)

BROOKLYN'S BAY RIDGE & FORT HAMILTON
A Photographic Journey 1870 -1970
by Brian Merlis & Lee Rosenzweig
165 pages   Landscape Format
ISBN 1-878741-45-4   **$29.95**   Hard Cover ($5.00 shipping)

BROOKLYN HEIGHTS & DOWNTOWN
Volume I 1860-1922
by Brian Merlis & Lee Rosenzweig   199 pages
ISBN 1-878741-51-9   **$29.95**   Hard Cover ($5.00 shipping)

STATEN ISLAND in OLD POST CARDS
by Brian Merlis & Bob Stonehill   150 Pages
ISBN 1878741-55-1   **$29.95**   (plus $5.00 shipping)

SPANNING THE NARROWS
Construction of the Verrazano-Narrows Bridge 1964-2004
by Brian Merlis & Lee Rosenzweig   80 pages
ISBN 1-87874161-6   **$24.95** Hard Cover ($5.00 shipping)

WELCOME BACK TO BOROUGH PARK
by Oscar Israelowitz & Brian Merlis   80 pages
ISBN 1878741-67-5   **$24.95** Hard Cover ($5.00 shipping)

SUBWAYS OF NEW YORK in VINTAGE PHOTOGRAPHS
by Oscar Israelowitz & Brian Merlis   245 pages
ISBN 1-878741-63-2   **$34.95**   Hard Cover ($5.00 shipping)

GUIDE TO JEWISH NEW YORK CITY
Celebrating 350 Years of Jewish Life in New York
by Oscar Israelowitz   245 pages
ISBN 1-878741-62-4   **$19.95** Paper (plus $5.00 shipping)

UNITED STATES JEWISH TRAVEL GUIDE (8th Edition)
by Oscar Israelowitz   380 pages
ISBN 1-878741-64-0   **$19.95** Paper (plus $5.00 shipping)

GUIDE TO JEWISH EUROPE -
Western Europe (10th Edition)
by Oscar Israelowitz   384 pages
ISBN 1-878741-19-5   **$19.95** Paper (plus $5.00 shipping)

ITALY JEWISH TRAVEL GUIDE
by Annie Sacerdoti   242 pages
ISBN 1-878741-42-X   **$19.95** Paper (plus $5.00 shipping)

JEWISH HERITAGE TRAIL OF NEW YORK
by Oscar Israelowitz   156 pages
ISBN 1-878741-60-8   **$19.95** Paper (plus $5.00 shipping)

ELLIS ISLAND GUIDE with Lower Manhattan
by Oscar Israelowitz   128 pages
ISBN 1-878741-01-2   **$7.95** Paper (plus $5.00 shipping)

SYNAGOGUES OF THE UNITED STATES
An Architectural & Photographic Survey
by Oscar Israelowitz   200 pages
ISBN 1-878741-09-8   **$24.95** Paper (plus $5.00 shipping)

SYNAGOGUES OF NEW YORK CITY
History of A Jewish Community
by Oscar Israelowitz   219 pages
ISBN 1-878741-44-6   **$35.00** Hard Cover ($5.00 shipping)

JEWISH NEW JERSEY in VINTAGE PHOTOGRAPHS
by Oscar Israelowitz   215 pages Landscape Format
ISBN 1-878741-59-4   **$29.95** Hard Cover ($5.00 shipping)

WELCOME BACK TO THE CATSKILLS
by Oscar Israelowitz   215 Pages Landscape Format
ISBN 1-878741-54-3   **$29.95** Hard Cover ($5.00 shipping)

ISRAELOWITZ PUBLISHING

P.O.Box 228   Brooklyn, NY 11229
Tel. (718) 951-7072
E-mail oscari 477 @aol.com
website: www.israelowitzpublishing.com

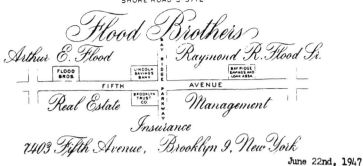

SHORE ROAD 5-3772

Flood Brothers

Arthur E. Flood   Raymond R. Flood Sr.

Real Estate   Management

Insurance

7403 Fifth Avenue, Brooklyn 9, New York

June 22nd, 1947

REMEMBER US ? OLD BAY RIDGEITES

ARMY   NAVY

The Floods, just out of the service, both born and raised in Bay Ridge, have returned to their native haunts to do what they have dreamed and planned during their wartime absence –

Arthur   OPEN OUR OWN PLACE OF BUSINESS   *Raymond*

So, we at last announce the opening, at a location convenient to the shopping and business center of Bay Ridge, of a modern, up-to-date Real Estate and Insurance Office equipped to take care of all your needs with a MAXIMUM of EFFICIENCY and a MINIMUM of WAITING

To our many friends, we need no introduction or recommendation – to those whom we have not served, ask our friends! No service is too great – no business too trivial. We founded our already existing insurance business on SERVICE, SINCERITY, and LOYALTY - WE SHALL CONTINUE THAT POLICY. TRY US – IN ANY EVENT, LET'S GET ACQUAINTED !!

    We offer to the general public our knowledge and experience over a long period of years in the field of insurance - FIRE, LIFE, CASUALTY - we write a full line of bonds. Regardless of whether you have a risk to be insured, if you merely seek information and advice, we will generously give you our time and service and plan with you your proper insurance protection.

    We are, as we have said, natives of Bay Ridge. However, in the Real Estate Field, we are not confining ourselves to specializing in Bay Ridge Properties. If you are in the market to buy, sell, rent or lease, we will give your problem utmost attention and consideration. If you are interested in Custom Built Homes, consult us first.

Very truly yours,

FLOOD BROS.

Arthur E. Flood
Raymond R. Flood

Flood Company
Licensed Real Estate Brokers

Raymond R. Flood, Jr., President
James F. Clark, Vice President

7403 - 5th Avenue
Brooklyn, New York 11209-2710
(718) 238-9800 Fax (718) 921-3020
Internet: http://www.floodcompany.com

FIFTY PLUS YEARS LATER...
FIFTY PLUS YEARS LATER...

WE REMAIN THE

PREMIER REAL ESTATE

AND INSURANCE OFFICE

IN

BAY RIDGE!

James F. Clark   *Raymond R. Flood Jr.*

JAMES F. CLARK, GRI   **RAYMOND R. FLOOD, JR.**
VICE PRESIDENT   **PRESIDENT**

REALTOR   EQUAL HOUSING OPPORTUNITY   MLS

A RESPECTED NAME IN THE PROFESSION.

1948

2006

1948

HAYM SALOMON HOME
FOR NURSING AND REHABILITATION
2340 CROPSEY AVENUE, BROOKLYN, NEW YORK

AMENITIES

- New State of the Art Facility
- All New Furnishings
- First Class Private and Semi Private Rooms
- Beautiful Sitting Rooms on All Floors
- Beauty/Barber Shop
- Outdoor Patio
- Spectacular Ocean Views

SERVICES

- 3 Gourmet Kosher Meals, Therapeutic Diets
- Creative Therapeutic Recreation Program
- In House Physician, All Subspecialties
- Comprehensive Social Services
- Pastoral Services
- Multilingual Staff
- Special Events and Entertainment

SPECIALIZING IN

- Short Term Rehabilitation:
  - Physical, Occupational and Speech Therapy
- Dementia Care
- Sub-Acute Care including:
  - Wound Care
  - Infusion/Oxygen Therapy
  - Pain Management/Hospice Care
  - Total Parenteral Nutrition
  - Tube Feedings
  - Tracheostomy/Colostomy/Ileostomy

For information about our services and programs or to schedule a tour call our Admissions Department:
(718) 535-9502

HAYM SALOMON...
when you need us we are here 24 hours a day, 7 days a week 365 days a year!

website: www.haymsalomonhomefornursingandrehabilitation.com

WWW.GIFTEDTWIST.COM

specializing in handmade quality crafts from around the world

all occasion gifts
home decor
antique prints
Jewelry, books and more

established 2003 in Staten Island NYC   info@giftedtwist.com 718-442-0762

"Your Bridge to the Past"

BROOKLYNPIX.com

Since 1980 Brooklyn Collectibles has provided the finest in archival photographs, maps, prints, and other items related to the history of Brooklyn, Manhattan, the outer boroughs, and surrounding areas. If you would like to own actual photographic prints or posters of images in this book, feel free to contact us. eBay seller name: BK.SALES

For leasing terms, conditions, and additional information, please email or call.
We gladly pay top dollar for better photographs, negatives and related historical materials.

Brian Merlis, president   Email: oldbrooklynphoto@aol.com
516-808-1214
516-623-3113

Lee A. Rosenzweig, associate
516-292-8677

maps • LIRR • books • medals • prints • relics • badges • plates • objects • atlases • tickets • buttons • ribbons • artwork • politics • ephemera
souvenirs • brochures • negatives • genealogy • histories • viewbooks • documents • paintings • billheads • broadsides • scrapbooks • handbills
post cards • newspapers • autographs • timetables • letterheads • advertising • photographs • Long Island • Dodger items • business cards
stock certificates • transportation • trade cards, &c.

HISTORICAL RESEARCH DONE   HISTORICAL PHOTOGRAPHS PROVIDED